WIMBLEDON 2011

THE CHAMPIONSHIPS
WIMBLEDON
OFFICIAL ANNUAL 2011

NEIL HARMAN

Publisher
PPL Sport & Leisure

Managing Director
Bill Cotton

Art Editor
David Kelly

Design Team
Emma Robinson
Graham Nuttall
Caroline O'Donovan

Photography
PA Photos

Editorial
Neil Harman

This edition
published 2011 by
PPL Sport & Leisure
16 Dempster Building
Atlantic Way
Brunswick Business Park
Liverpool L3 4BE

PPL Sport & Leisure
Bradford House
East Street
Epsom, Surrey KT17 1BL

ISBN 978-1-903381-22-9
Printed by Scotprint
East Lothian EH41 3ST

CONTENTS

FOREWORD
Philip Brook

Chairman of The All England Lawn Tennis and Croquet Club
and Committee of Management of The Championships

The first Wimbledon Championships were played in 1877. At that time The All England Croquet and Lawn Tennis Club, as the Club was then known, needed to raise funds for the repair of the broken pony roller – essential for the upkeep of croquet lawns – and to this end decided to hold a tennis tournament. From a field of 22 British players, Spencer Gore was victorious and received prize money of 12 guineas. 200 spectators paid to watch the final.

Fast forward to the 125th Championships and some things haven't changed. Grass tennis courts, white tennis clothing, five set matches for men and the tournament still played in Wimbledon. Today these represent some of the most important traditions of The Championships.

Some things have changed, however. This year our new singles champions, Novak Djokovic and Petra Kvitova each received £1.1m in prize money. Their finals were each watched by 15,000 people on Centre Court and on television by tennis fans in over 185 countries worldwide. For the first time, Wimbledon was broadcast in '3D'. Competitors from 68 countries took part.

This year also saw the opening of new No. 3 Court, a 2,000 seater stadium equipped with Hawkeye technology. Wet weather on five days during The Championships meant that the Centre Court roof was given a serious work-out for the first time, thereby ensuring live world class tennis every day throughout the fortnight.

We were delighted to have Royalty attend The Championships on eleven days, with the highlight being a visit by the newly married Their Royal Highnesses The Duke and Duchess of Cambridge. Once again we welcomed back many former Wimbledon champions, with no fewer than ten former ladies' singles winners watching the ladies' final between Petra Kvitova and Maria Sharapova from the Royal Box.

So 124 Championships later, I wonder what Spencer would have made of things? Hopefully, he would be proud that those original traditions have been maintained. I think he would be amazed with the progress of The Championships and the innovations that have taken place.

I hope this annual will bring back many happy memories for you of the 125th Championships.

INTRODUCTION

Neil Harman,
The Times

The draw for 125th edition of Wimbledon had reached a bit of a dull passage when Andrew Jarrett, the referee said "No.46 John Isner will play (pause for dramatic effect and a look at the coin in his left hand) No.78 Nicolas Mahut." The usually hushed theatre of the All England Club's main interview room was interrupted by belly laughs. In 125 years of the Championships, there had never been anything like it.

The Twitter-sphere was lit up with "Oh My Gods" and "It's insane" and "You've got to be kidding me" and those of us in the room, having picked ourselves up from the floor began to prepare for "Isnut - The Return of the Marathon Men." As someone once said: "You could not make it up."

Before the first round of Wimbledon in 2010, Isner and Mahut barely knew each other, they had the occasional nodding acquaintance, they were like so many of the transients of tennis who come and go and sometimes find themselves on the opposite side of a court and get on with it

It happened to the pair of them last year, a first round match that appeared, on the face of it, to bear little consequence until they served, served, served and served some more until they could barely stand and after 11 hours and 5 minutes (the time of a flight from London to Los Angeles) across three days, acres of newsprint and loss of commentators' voices, a backhand pass from Isner won the day(s).

When they were chained together again for the first round this year, the chances were, according to the referee who knows these things, 111 squared. Someone else reckoned it was a 1 in 142.5 chance (or 0.7%) There was a two in three chance for Isner to have avoided a seed in the opening round and a one in 95 chance of Mahut being placed in the slot next to him. Mahut was in the locker room when the draw was being made, and his attention was drawn when an attendant gasped "Oh no" "What's up?" he asked. "You're playing Isner again," came the reply.

Never had one match so dominated conversation, both at the Club and throughout the world. Isner said he had been trying to put the match behind him and realised that, in the plucking of a coin from a velvet bag, it was right there in front of him again.

Mahut had written a book called the *Match of My Life* with Philippe Bouin, the former chief tennis writer for *L'Equipe*. In it, he spoke of the second day of the match "After my second ice-bath, Pierre [the fitness trainer] went to bed. Boris [Villejo, Mahut's coach] stayed up trying to distract me by teaching me the Rubik's Cube. It didn't work. I finally went back to my room at 1.30am, and got a few hours' sleep. Three or four, no more. The next morning I was late on court because I had a nosebleed, something that had never happened to me before. We played for an hour, and then, at 68-69, I faced match point for the first time. I wasn't frightened. I served at his body, he returned, and I saw my half-volley climbing and climbing towards his side of the court. I knew he would try to pass me down the line. He always passed me down the line. I had even put that in the notes on my Blackberry.

"But my legs wouldn't respond, and the ball flew past my nose. It was at once very fast and very slow. It was the end of the world." And now they had to do it all over again.

It was no surprise that one match dominated conversation as we approached the grounds to celebrate another magnificent Wimbledon milestone. But, elsewhere, the games were being stepped up, the courts being cut, the food and drink prepared, the uniforms being dusted down, the seats dusted and the cameras and computers being readied for another momentous two weeks.

Of course, local focus landed four square on the shoulders of Andy Murray, as it had been for the last four years at this time. Having arrived on the back of another victory at Queen's Club and after his finest ever French Open showing – a semi-final defeat to the eventual champion, Rafael Nadal, we had our stories all ready to go.

A pre-tournament interview with the BBC's *Sportsweek* programme, put his hopes into optimistic perspective. Murray said he was taking his diet more seriously, his training had become more specific, he was having fun working out, he was taking more responsibility for himself, to the extent of taking blood tests to determine whether he was getting the best from his body. These were decisive steps. But could he possibly win a championship like this, simply by lowering his tone, through restraint and reining in – especially if it was raining out?

"What is difficult for me when I'm on the court in that pressure situation and the stress levels are at their highest, is that you're likely to say something you don't mean, or get angry and upset," the 24-year-old two-time semi-finalist said. "In my last two matches at Queen's especially, I felt really calm, I got pumped up at the right time and I wasn't using up too much energy. That's something I definitely need to improve on. I need to get better at it and I will."

The women's event had been given belated sharp focus with the decision of the Williams sisters to return to competitive tennis. Venus had played only Grand Slam tournaments since last year's Championships; Serena had not even done that, for she lacerated her foot on glass in a German restaurant in July and then, after criss-crossing the United States by air, she felt unwell, was taken to hospital and it was discovered that a blood clot had moved from her leg onto her lung. There was no time to waste. An operation was essential.

After all that, was tennis still worth it? I bumped into the girls' father, Richard, on the prom at Eastbourne the week before The Championships. "I try not to think about them winning," he told me. "I have seen so many parents put so much pressure on their kids and coaches putting so much pressure on the players. I was training them for something that they could do, to be extraordinary at tennis. And while they were playing, I wanted them to make the transition (to another life) smoothly. I'm happy if they win and happy if they lose. Either way it's going to be okay with me. And I think that's why I'm such good friends with them. I don't want to be known as a tennis dad, as a tennis father. I just want to be their father. That's enough for me.

"I was telling someone this morning I'm a professional ball picker-upper. I smile a lot with them, I laugh and joke with them, especially if they are having a bad day in practice. A lot of that carries over when you go play too. I often ask them 'what would you do if you had to play yourself?' If you can get them to think maybe, just maybe, they can go win."

Having seen his daughters win so much, what did their father make of his own story – the heart of a champion? "It's confidence, a lot of confidence," he said. "A person who loves themselves and believes in themselves is able to accomplish no matter what the conditions are, it makes no difference to them. I write notes to my kids and ask them 'at this tournament, what did you do to win?' You try to get them to think. I would never tell them 'you did this, you did that' I don't do that because if you think for someone they won't think when they go play."

Because of the distinct grass court formula used by the club to determine its seedings, Serena had been promoted from No.26 in the rankings to the No.7 seeded position (she was No.8 but had gone up a place when Kim Clijsters, the world No.2 from Belgium, said she had to withdraw with a hip injury).

The day before the curtain rose, Mick Desmond, the Club's new commercial director, revealed that the Wimbledon website (wimbledon.com) had just registered its second million in terms of unique users and the tournament app had gone to No.1 in the charts. There was simply no stopping the success story of SW19. Everyone, it seemed, wanted to be involved.

With no football championship during the fortnight, with Rory McIlroy, from Northern Ireland, having won the US Open golf title on the day before the Club gates were open (Conor Niland was the first Irishman to land in Wimbledon's main draw since Matt Doyle in 1983 from success in the qualifying competition), with everything in its place, we chugged down Church Road again on the 20th of June with hope in our hearts and the thought of who would be the ones fulfilling their destinies in the 14 days that lie ahead?

LIVE FOR

TIME MARCHES ON. YET WIMBLEDON REMAINS
UNCHANGED. ITS TRADITIONS AND GROUNDS
REVERED, THE HONOUR BELONGS TO THE
PLAYERS AND SPECTATORS ALIKE. THE WORDS
"FOREVER LEGENDARY" ARE NOT WRITTEN
ON THE GATES OF WIMBLEDON, BUT THEY DO
EXIST IN THE AIR.

GREATNESS

OYSTER PERPETUAL DAY-DATE

Rafael Nadal
Seeded 1st
Age: 25 Born: Manacor, Majorca, Spain

He was to be afforded the right of stepping out to defend his Wimbledon crown for the first time. Having missed The 2009 Championships through injury, he was not able to relish the experience of leading the first day parade on Centre the year after his momentous triumph in 2008. In the meantime, Nadal had taken his Grand Slam tally to 10, with victories in last year's US Open – he was denied the 'Rafa Slam' when beaten in the quarter-finals at the Australian Open by fellow Spaniard David Ferrer – and for the sixth time, he was triumphant on the clay of Roland Garros, to which he added the titles in Monte Carlo and Barcelona. A loss to Jo-Wilfried Tsonga at Queen's was written off because he felt he had had enough practice on grass.

Roger Federer
Seeded 2nd
Age: 29 Born: Basel, Switzerland

Having arrived at The 2010 Championships with 16 Grand Slam titles, he had been unable to add to his haul in the meantime, which either said that he had reached a bit of an impasse or the rest were slowly catching up the with the Meister. Federer had chosen to sidestep any formal grass court competition between reaching the final of the French Open, where he won the first set in scintillating style against Rafael Nadal but could not quite retain that level enough to deny the Spaniard. There had been a couple of rum defeats for Federer in the past year though he did capture the Barclays ATP World Tour title at the 02 in November which many thought would be the launch-pad for another spellbinding year.

Novak Djokovic
Seeded 3rd
Age: 24 Born: Belgrade, Serbia

He entered Wimbledon for the seventh time – two semi-final appearances had been his best achievement – on the back of a start to the year which made history at every turn. Having reached the final of last year's US Open, he held a lot back to turn his attention to the Davis Cup Final where he led Serbia to an inaugural triumph. From then on, there was no stopping this ferociously committed right hander who won a second Australian Open, successive ATP Masters 1000 events in Indian Wells, Miami, Madrid and Rome, accumulating 41 consecutive victories in the year before he was knocked out of the French in the semi-finals by Roger Federer. It had been quite an extraordinary period.

Andy Murray
Seeded 4th
Age: 24 Born: Dunblane, Scotland

The see-saw experience of covering the Scot's career showed little sign of calming down any time soon. He ended 2010 as the world No.4 for the third straight year, highlighted by a victory in Shanghai, when he demolished Roger Federer in the final. If he could only play like that every week. A second consecutive appearance in the Australian Open final but it was to be like the first, a straight sets defeat, this time to Novak Djokovic. He crashed to difficult defeats on the US hard court surface but picked his form up spectacularly on clay, reaching the semi-finals in Monte Carlo, Rome and, for the first time, Roland Garros. A victory at Queen's Club the week before Wimbledon added to the frenzy of speculation.

Robin Soderling
Seeded 5th
Age: 26 Born: Tibro, Sweden

For quite a reserved person – as befits being Swedish - Soderling's career had taken quite a few twists and turns in the past year, as he parted company with Magnus Norman, his coach, at the end of 2010, decided to start working with Claudio Pistolesi, the Italian and then decided he did not like that combination so went back to his native country and persuaded Freddie Rosengren to give up his media career to return to full time coaching. He won the tournaments in Marseille and Rotterdam in February but could not seem to make it beyond the fourth round of the bigger events, losing there at three clay court events in succession, including Roland Garros where he lost in straight sets to Rafael Nadal. He did not play on grass before The Championships.

Tomas Berdych
Seeded 6th
Age: 26 Born: Valasske Mezirici, Czech Republic

When Berdych reached the 2010 final – defeating Roger Federer in the quarter-finals *en route* - it was as much of a surprise to him as anyone else and he found it hard to live up to the expectations it raised. He also finished the year inside the world's top ten for the first time – though he had not won a title in the entire year having played more tournaments (10) than anyone else inside that elite - and debuted at the Barclays ATP World Tour Finals. Entering The Championships, he had not been to a final in 2011, either, the nearest being a couple of semi-final appearances in relatively minor events in Chennai, Dubai, Nice and Halle, Germany which at least showed he had some grass court form under his belt before returning to SW19.

David Ferrer

Seeded 7th

Age: 29 Born: Javea, Spain

Being No.2 at anything in any country would be the cause for wild celebration but David Ferrer had become used to living in the shadows of Rafael Nadal. He went about his work diligently and fearlessly, largely from the back of the court where he never lacked for stamina. Started the year with a victory in Auckland and took Andy Murray to four sets in the semi-finals of the Australian Open and reached two finals on clay, in Monte Carlo and Barcelona, losing both to the aforementioned Nadal. At the French Open, Ferrer reached the fourth round before losing 8-6 in the final set to Gael Monfils in an absorbing match. He also decided to miss any grass court competition ahead of Wimbledon.

Andy Roddick

Seeded 8th

Age: 28. Born: Omaha, Nebraska, USA

Roddick was bounced into the top eight seeding position because of his performances on grass over the past few years and indeed, he merited such a rise in status. No one had given more, tried harder or worked more diligently than the American former world No.1. He had completed a ninth straight year as a top ten player in December, joining Roger Federer among active players to achieve the feat. He started the year in coruscating style, winning the Brisbane title and following that up in Memphis on indoor hard court but he hurt his shoulder in the clay court season and was forced to abandon plans to compete in the French Open. Nevertheless, he had reached the semi-finals on grass at Queen's where he was a four-time champion so did not lack for confidence.

Caroline Wozniacki

Seeded 1st

Age 20 Born: Odense, Denmark

How hard was it for a reigning No.1 to talk and act as if she belonged in that position when all everyone wanted to know was if she would ever win a Grand Slam tournament? Wozniacki handled it all pretty well considering. She won a WTA Tour – leading six titles in 2010 (the most by any player in a season since Justine Henin won 10 in 2007) and became the youngest to rise to No.1 since Maria Sharapova in 2005. Her US Open final appearance though, in 2009, remained the standard she could not quite replicate. A match point against Li Na in the semi-finals of the Australian Open went begging and though she took her tournament title tally to 17 in Copenhagen the week before Wimbledon, she was still not highly considered among potential favourites

Vera Zvonareva

Seeded 2nd

Age: 26 Born: Moscow, Russia

The beaten finalist of 2010 advanced also to the final of the US Open in September, where she was beaten by Kim Clijsters and to four others besides on the WTA Tour so there was no doubting the durability of the latest Russian to show prowess at the higher echelons on tennis. As a fascinating stat, she did not lose a single tie-break she played in 2010. In 2011, she had been to the semi-finals of the Australian Open, where Clijsters again stood in her way and clinched her 11th title in Dubai, defeating Wozniacki in the final. Her grinding style meant she would always be there or thereabouts and was a quarter-finalist at Eastbourne the week before The Championships, before losing to Australia's Samantha Stosur.

Li Na
Seeded 3rd
Age: 29 Born: Wuhan, China

She led the news bulletins in China after becoming the first player from her country to win a Grand Slam title, doing so in Paris where she defeated the defending champion Franscesca Schiavone in the final. Suddenly everyone wanted to know all they could about this charming Chinese, who had thrown off the shackles of the rigid rules of her country and broken out into the wide world in remarkable fashion. We should have been warned, for she had reached her first Grand Slam final in Australia in January, losing to Kim Clijsters. Not surprisingly she had a little dip after that in result terms, losing four 1st rounds but rebounded to reach the semi-finals in Madrid and Rome before her extravagant breakthrough at Roland Garros.

Victoria Azarenka
Seeded 4th
Age: 21 Born: Minsk, Belarus

Would this be the tournament when the delightful 21-year-old from Minsk took a bold step into the unknown and reached a Grand Slam semi-final for the first time? She had finished 2010 inside the top ten for a second consecutive year and the turning point in the spring had come at the Sony Ericsson Open in Miami, when she won the title, playing superbly confident tennis to defeat Maria Sharapova in the final (and taking out Kim Clijsters and Vera Zvonareva en route). Azarenka had a tendency to fall foul of injuries, having to retire in Stuttgart with shoulder problems and after losing to eventual champion Li Na in Paris, she retired in the Eastbourne quarter-finals the week before Wimbledon to rest an injured thigh muscle.

Maria Sharapova
Seeded 5th

Age: 24 Born: Nyagan, Russia

To find Sharapova back in the mix as one of the top seeds was a remarkable testament to her fighting spirit. After shoulder surgery in 2008, she gritted her teeth and fought her way back into contention. She was the only player at last year's Wimbledon to have a set point against eventual champion Serena Williams. A viral illness meant that the early part of her 2011 campaign was cut short but after a semi-final appearance in Indian Wells and reaching the final in Miami, she was restored to the top 10. She won her 23rd tour title in Rome and was a semi-finalist in Paris, where Li Na stopped her in her tracks. Sharapova chose not to play in the grass court warm up event at Birmingham to prepare in private for The Championships.

Francesca Schiavone
Seeded 6th

Age: 30 Born: Milan, Italy

We still relished the livewire Italian for her 2010 French Open title and she almost repeated a year later, reaching the final where only the efficiency of Li Na ground her down. It was a superb renaissance from the now 30-year-old who proved that age was definitely no barrier to success. She had been involved in the best women's match of the year, a 4 hour and 44 minute fourth round match against Svetlana Kuznetsova in the Australian Open, which she won 16-14 in the final set. She still had enough left to give Wozniacki a run for her money in the quarters but lost in three sets. For the most part she was involved in the latter stages of every tournament she entered but still did not have the greatest feel for the grass.

Serena Williams
Seeded 7th

Age: 29 Born: Saginaw, Michigan, USA

We did not know until the very last minute whether the four-time champion from the United States would be able to make it at all in 2011. The story of her past 12 months had been on of freak injury, near fatal illness, dogged determination and now we were ready to welcome both her and Venus, her sister, back to the fold. Serena had played one tournament since last year's Championships, in Eastbourne the week before at the AEGON International, in which she lost the first five games to Tsvetana Pironkova of Bulgaria, recovered to win but could not defeat Vera Zvonareva in the second round. Even given her talents, she was bound to be rusty. Though she was ranked No.26 on the tour, she was bounced up the list given her grass court pedigree

Petra Kvitova
Seeded 8th

Age: 21 Born: Bilovec, Czech Republic

Having never played a grass court match in her life until last year's Championships, where she reached the semi-finals, a lot of shrewd judges felt this could be the left hander's time. After Wimbledon last year, she had suffered a run of five straight tournament losses and thus finished the year ranked No.34 on the WTA Tour. Her 2011 campaign had been a sequence of stories of withdrawals and retirements through injury but she had won her fourth tour title in the major event in Madrid on clay and reached the fourth round at the French, beaten by Li Na. Those looking for a Wimbledon portent were encouraged when Kvitova reached the final at Eastbourne, played two days before The Championships, where she was beaten by Marion Bartoli of France.

dreas BECK	**v**	Andy RODDICK
lek STEPANEK	**v**	Fernando VERDASC
ena JANKOVIC	**v**	Maria Jose MARTINEZ SANCH
asia PAVLYUCHENKOVA	**v**	Lesia TSURENK
ra ZAHLAVOVA STRYCOVA	**v**	Aleksandra WOZNIA
ecca MARINO	**v**	Patricia MAYR-ACHLEITN
-ChenCHANG	**v**	Marina ERAKOV
ela HANTUCHOVA	**v**	Vitalia DIATCHENK
ania MIRZA	**v**	Virginie RAZZAN
na FALCONI	**v**	Stephanie DUBO

18

DAY ONE
20.06.2011

O'Brien
vs
Date-Krumm

Nadal
vs
Russell

Young
vs
Bogomolov

V. Williams
vs
Amanmuradova

A. Murray
vs
Gimeno-Traver

Bellucci
vs
Scheuttler

MONDAY 20TH JUNE...

For the second time in three years, non-tennis-shoe-shod footsteps made their way across a new piece of Wimbledon turf on day one of the Championships. In 2009, the Duke of Kent, President of the All England Club christened the new No.2 Court; this time he had moved on to cut the ribbon on the embryonic No.3. It is a wonderful court but for those of us of a certain vintage, the current No.1 will never replace the old No.1, nor will No.2 or No.3 replace the old No.2. But we cannot halt the march of progress.

Whatever our sentiments may be, there is no mistaking the perfection of the design, and that it fitted in so well with the general ambience of the club. One of the many remarkable elements of Wimbledon is that whatever they have done to reshape the grounds across the years, all has happened with a touch of distinction.

As Laura Robson was given first rub of the No.2 green two years ago, so it was Katie O'Brien, from Yorkshire, who was accorded

The Duke of Kent opens the new look Court 3 prior to the match between Great Britain's Katie O'Brien (left) and Japan's Kimiko Date-Krumm

The new Court No. 3

the pleasure of striking the opening ball on No.3. In fact, for 17 minutes, she barely laid glove on the ball at all, as Japan's Kimiko Date-Krumm, 40 (that's her age, not her ranking) won the first set without relinquishing a game. Date-Krumm was to win 6-0 7-5 to leave O'Brien bereft and heading to Henman Hill for a recuperative glass of Pimm's with her friends.

Of the many improvements to the grounds at Wimbledon, what did the six-time champion Roger Federer (and someone whom the club regarded as a friend as well as a member) say? "I feel like they are ahead of their time," he said. "They are still looking at ways to make it more fan friendly, more media friendly, more player friendly." He said he could see huge potential for further growth in the coming years if the club could use the adjacent property for further development.

"Who knows, maybe in 30 years they will have the qualifying tournament here," he said, referring to the fact that Wimbledon was the only one of the four Grand Slam tournaments which staged their 'rehearsal' off site, at the Bank of England Grounds in Roehampton. "They have so much potential to grow here, it seems like they are doing all the right things, except knocking down your (not his, you notice) Court No.2, the graveyard."

In truth, if you weren't a romantic keenly attuned to the lost links with past champions, past matches, past horror stories, it was possible to sit inside the new Court 3 and notice it was quite a cosy, comfortable place.

"I'd played on the old Court 2," O'Brien said. "It was a little bit similar but it was more intimate on Court 3. I think it's going to turn out to be one of the players' favourite courts to play on." About her loss, she was asked if it ➤

Kimiko Date-Krumm

was still worth it, all this playing and losing? "I have days like that definitely, but I guess there are people who would be dying to have played at Wimbledon as many times as I have."

Strolling back from No.3, I caught sight of Sebastien Nadal and Ana Maria Parera, Rafa's mum and dad dolled up to the nines. They were to be treated to the full range of the All England Club's cordiality. Mum had flown in especially for the occasion and was leaving the following morning to return to Majorca. They enjoyed lunch, especially the coffee and chocolates, one was told, and once again, Wimbledon had struck the perfect chord.

The first day on Centre was always a touch tricky. The lawn, with lines so true it seemed as if each mower was fitted with its own spirit level, is almost too nice. Nadal was moved that not only he could play on 'this perfect court,' but that his parents would be afforded such an opportunity to see him play on a pristine patch.

"I have never seen a court as beautiful as this," he said after his 6-4 6-2 6-2 victory over Michael Russell, an American who started with a bang and was reduced in the end to diving around like Boris Becker in his dirt-stained days in an attempt to prolong the points. "This is the best match to be seen from such a position. It was a big emotion for me and a thrill for them and I'm thankful they were given such an opportunity."

In the recent past, champions such as Federer and Pete Sampras have walked out

Rafael Nadal
(above) and
Michael Russell

on the opening day and have departed again with barely a detectable footprint to confirm that they were ever there. This is not the Nadal way. A couple of times he appeared to look down at the turf as if apologetic that he should be tearing it up but then again, as he said, he does not play as if both of his feet have left the ground *a la* Federer, he paws at it as would a bull about to do extremely nasty things to a matador.

There was no Sampras-like leviathan for America in the men's draw. Their tournament started with a midday meeting of the two men – Donald Young and Alex Bogomolov Jnr – who had defeated Andy Murray in the first round of the Masters 1000 tournaments in Indian Wells and Miami in March. Both

had hovered around the top 100, although watching Bogomolov win in four sets, one was tempted to see the result as decisive proof of the depths of Murray's doldrums at the time.

At least Court 17 seemed a poignant location for a display of American grass-court tennis 2011 vintage, lodged in the shadows of Centre and No.1, its seating so shallow that passers by lean in at the edges like neighbours craning across a garden hedge. At one stage Bogomolov lost his grip on his racket and sent it hurtling over the midget-level rear awning and clattering onto the Tarmac walkway outside, narrowly missing a pedestrian.

There were no stars and stripes flags here, not even a celebratory whoop or yowl or "Yoo! Ess! Ay!" as the backwards-capped Bogomolov broke in the second set to shift the momentum of the match. Young, a lovely ➤

Alex Bogomolov Jnr

mover possessed of an elegant backhand slice, is seen as a little fragile and so it proved in the face of his more aggressive compatriot. Bogomolov won 7-5 4-6 6-3 6-1.

There was another, rather more recognisable American on Court No.2, though in attire we hadn't seen before. Venus Williams has had enough time between recent engagements to come up with something rather special on her return to Wimbledon – only two tournaments since last year's event – and is a pretty dab hand with the embroidery needle but her lace outfit as she stepped out to face Ukbekistan's Akgul Amanmuradova drew the undivided attention of the photographers massing

Williams won 6-3 6-1. Giles Smith of *The Times* noted that 'the only person who showed any sign of first day nerves was one of the ballboys when imperiously handed the plastic wrapping from Williams's racket. He emitted an almost audible gulp of panic and looked for guidance from the umpire, who coolly advised him to dispose of it in the bin. It was impossible to blame him for anxiety and confusion – imagine binning Williams's wrapper, only to discover she was intending to wear it later!'

And so to Mr Murray and the centrepiece of the evening which would see him play his first round match against the Spaniard, Daniel Gimeno-Traver. As if on cue, Scottish conditions prevailed. It had started to rain, so the roof that had lain almost dormant for the past two years was drawn across. It would be only the second time, after his fourth round against Stanislas Wawrinka in 2009, that the British No.1 would play on an indoor grass court.

Maybe he still could not get used to the unsettling feeling that, just when he was ready to play on the greatest court in the greatest outdoor tournament in the sport, suddenly he was asked to go to work in a building which felt like a cross between the Kew Gardens Temperate House and a run-of-the-mill Dutch indoor arena.

➤ Venus Williams

Andy Murray

Daniel Gimeno-Traver

The atmosphere was somewhat muted. The crowds had been down a thousand on the previous year's first day and the Club had ruled, rightly, that the match could not be shown on the slopes near No.1 Court because they were too slippery. Memories of not so happy times for Murray in the spring abounded.

It was, to say the least, a curious match, conducted in near reverential silence until it became apparent that the sacrificial lamb had turned into a bit of a lion. As the rain arrived earlier than forecast, the faithful huddled in the warm glow of their sheltered place of worship to watch the Scot deal with a trickier than expected assignment and advance to the second round in two hours and eight minutes, dropping the first set, hanging in to snatch the second, then destroying the Spaniard in the final two sets without losing a game.

In the face of his opponent's inspired resistance, followed by a collapse that worsened after Gimeno-Traver had treatment for a leg injury, Murray gathered his resources to win 4-6 6-3 6-0 6-0. He dropped only 15 points in the last two sets and though he had played better in recent weeks and would do so again – we hoped – in this tournament, it was a clean start. For the moment he was satisfied to have turned a stern test into a walkover.

At the end Murray was playing some glorious stuff against an opponent who had briefly entertained thoughts of the biggest victory of his otherwise anonymous career, hitting hard and clean from the baseline, enjoying the freedom afforded all outsiders.

Still, even in his most threatening moments, Gimeno-Traver did not look like an opponent who could sustain such excellence – although Murray was adamant that he had at no stage taken him lightly.

The most prominent men's seed to lose on the first day was the young Brazilian left hander Thomaz Bellucci (No.30) who had enjoyed a successful clay court campaign but would need more time to get the measure of grass. He was beaten 7-6 6-4 6-2 by Rainer Scheuttler of Germany, the 2008 semi-finalist.

QUOTE of the Day

Andy Murray, who was woken up at 7.00am three days before The Championships for a doping test.

"I looked at my clock and it was bang on 7 o'clock. I knew it was them. He rang the bell six times. My mum did make them (the testers) a cup of tea, but we shouldn't do that apparently. It's very intrusive when you get someone in your house in the morning, when you're going to the toilet and they're staring at you. It's quite a strange feeling."

DAY TWO
21.06.2011

Niland
vs
Mannarino

Evans
vs
Mayer

Cox
vs
Stakhovsky

Ward
vs
Llodra

Isner
vs
Mahut

S. Williams
vs
Rezai

Federer
vs
Kukushkin

Conor Niland

TUESDAY 21ST JUNE...

There were 1,109 folk in the queue to watch the second day's play at The Championships and there was plenty of local interest on the outside courts to keep them happy. Actually, if watching Brits was your fancy it always paid to arrive early to avoid disappointment but otherwise there were such magical names as Dominguez Lino; Haider-Maurer; Roger-Vasselin; Devvarman, Berlocq; Yakimova, Pospisil or Dubois to watch. Did we not just love days like these?

Nothing in tennis matches a stroll through the grounds in the first week at Wimbledon. Okay they can be a bit of a pain as someone steps on the back of your heel, you feel the sharp prod of an umbrella, you never quite seem to get to one of the benches before they are filled and someone moves across your vision just as a critical shot is played. To me, it beats the press seats on Court No.1 all ends up.

Early in the day, I was in the crush at Court No.5, to watch Dan Evans, of Britain, facing Florian Mayer, the German who plays 'rubbish' tennis shots better than anyone in the world; and some eight hours later, it was hard to get a space around No.17 as Conor Niland, of Ireland, took on Adrian Mannarino, of France. What one could see was utterly absorbing.

Niland, from Limerick and the first Irishman to compete in the main draw for quite some time was 4-1 up in the final set, just two games away from a date with Roger Federer in the second round of the biggest tennis tournament in the world. He said that at that stage he began to think of the court over his left shoulder rather than the one he was currently standing on and that was the problem. Perhaps he rather enjoyed the sensational backhand crosscourt pass he produced on the point to grant him a two-break lead and dwelt on it a touch too long.

Though he was giving over a huge ranking disparity – from No.181 in the world against the No.55 – Niland had been more than a match for his opponent, displaying all the dogged determination and ne'er say die attitude that had marked his progress over the years.

According to Jonny Watterson in *The Irish Times* "It has become a Jesuitical point but Niland was the first Irish male player to appear in the Wimbledon main draw since Californian-born Matt Doyle in 1984. Doyle played Davis Cup for Ireland in 1983 but according to various opinion did not have an Irish passport until 1985. It raises the conundrum as to whether Doyle was Irish in 1985 but American in 1984. Still, Sean Sorensen, from Cork, played here in 1980 and Niland's appearance bridges more than two decades without an Irish presence." I think we'll leave it at that.

Clearly, when approaching the four-hour mark Niland faltered, made some unforced errors of which Mannarino took full advantage, winning the final set and the match 4-6 6-4 7-6 4-6 6-4 after exactly four hours. "It was the biggest match of my career, and to have it ➤

33

so close, for sure I'll think about over the next few days," said the 29-year-old, in a moment of Rafael Nadal-like straightforwardness.

"At the moment I don't feel as bad as I probably thought I would, but I don't know. Closing out matches is the most important thing and I do feel I let myself down a little bit in terms of putting myself in a position where I shouldn't really have let it slip. I do feel a little bit disappointed in myself that I didn't find a way to win it."

As for Evans, he joined James Ward and Dan Cox in losing in the singles, which meant that Andy Murray was left friendless in the men's singles for another year. Evans was beaten 7-6 7-6 3-6 6-4 and, as one could tell by the closeness of the scoreline, he had his moments when he gave a top 30 player plenty of trouble.

Neither Ward, who had reached the semi-finals of the AEGON Championships at Queen's nor Cox were able to garner a set; Sergiy Stakhovsky, of Ukraine taking care of Cox 6-2 6-4 and Ward was beaten 6-3 7-6 6-3 by a very tricky customer in Michael Llodra, the Frenchman, and No.19 seed.

Leon Smith, the head of men's tennis at the LTA said: "When you look at the rankings of our guys compared to their opponents it was an extremely difficult task. For all of the British players it is about feeling the level, making the most of the experience and really pushing on in the Challenger tournaments in the weeks ahead." In other words, the same old story.

There was a sense of *déjà vu* on Court No.3 where they would stage the re-match of 'The Match'. There had been intense debate as to where John Isner and Nicolas Mahut would cross swords once more. The sentimentalists wanted it to be back on 18 with Mohamed Lahyani, the umpire in the chair, but it seemed inappropriate to try to completely replicate what had happened a year ago. Better to make a fresh start and the committee decided the best place was the freshest court, the new No.3.

Of course it wouldn't be the same, it couldn't be. Mahut had allowed a writer from *L'Equipe*, the French sports newspaper, to spend precisely 11 hours and five minutes with him on Sunday, exactly the length of the 2010 extravaganza, a piece of great thinking by the paper and to which Mahut's positive response showed just what a good sport, as well as superb tennis player, he is. The match had to be a damp squib, everyone said it would be as, to all intents and purposes, it was. To cut a long story short, Isner won (again) but this time by the rather more conventional 7-6 6-2 7-6, in a match described by many as a very ordinary, every day defeat. And short, too.

It was dry with a few wispy clouds over Court No.3 but on Centre, my goodness it was chucking it down. But not in that way. Serena Williams was coming over all dewy-eyed after she marked her return to a court she loved so much with a 6-3 3-6 6-1 victory over Aravane Rezai of France. It was exactly the same kind

of topsy-turvy match as had been her first at Eastbourne the previous week; giving notice that Serena, though definitely here in person, had a long way to go before she could assume dominance again.

"It definitely was so emotional for me because throughout the last 12 months I've been through, you know, a lot of things that are not normal, things you guys don't even know about," Williams said. "So it's just been a long, arduous road. To stand up is still pretty awesome." She had missed 11 months of competition after two operations to repair a torn tendon in her right foot and then a period in hospital to recover from blood clots in her lungs and a haematoma that required emergency treatment.

She has said here that she feared for her life at one stage, but she also said that she was always determined to return to the sport she has dominated intermittently since the early 2000s. Though struggling at times with her movement, her first-serve consistency and her returns, she also showed frequent flashes of vintage Williams: ripping forehand winners in extension and finishing with 13 aces, including one on the final point that brought on the sobs.

"It's been a disaster year, but you know I've been praying and I have my family and I love tennis, and to be able to come back at Wimbledon is pretty awesome," Williams said. "I didn't expect to play. I'm just excited. I never cried with joy for anything."

Watching all of this unfold from the Royal Box were members of England's Ashes winning cricket squad, captain Andrew Strauss, vice-captain Alistair Cook, Jonathan Trott, James Anderson and Graeme Swann to the fore. 'Swanny' – I hope he doesn't mind me calling him that – had become a bit of a tennis fan, having spent a few hours earlier this year spinning yarns and enthusing over the women's game at the Australian Open. Apparently, mistaking the lapel badge of an All England Club member for a waiter's insignia, he asked one prominent member on the committee if they'd mind replenishing his glass of wine on the balcony. It was all taken in excellent spirit.

The lads had really come to watch a bit of Roger Federer and three sets satisfied them – and the six time champion. The wind here messed around a bit with his hair but did not stop him making an impressive start to his quest to match Pete Sampras's haul of titles. Mikhail Kukushkin, of Kazakhstan, put up a pretty good fight, especially in the first set and a half, but Federer duly worked his way through the gears to ease into round two with a 7-6 6-4 6-2 victory.

It was a far cry from last year when the Swiss was staring at a first-round defeat, with Alejandro Falla, of Colombia, serving for the match in the fourth set of the opening match of the tournament. But the result was the same as Federer progressed and he even managed to throw in a bit of old fashioned

England Cricketers in the Royal Box

chip-charge – shades of Paul Annacone's influence- when things got a bit easier deep into the third set.

"I struggled early on in the first set to get any read on his serve, even though he's not the biggest server," Federer said. "He served consistently. But then I never really struggled on my serve and I was able to cruise, actually, through lots of my service games. Overall it was a good performance but conditions were tough; it was a really tricky wind out there."

Though Federer's wife, Mirka, was a professional player and used to be his manager, it is hard to imagine him agreeing to be coached by her, at least not seriously. Kukushkin has no such hang-ups and has been coached by his girlfriend, Anastasia Ulikhina, a physical education graduate, for the past two years. It is an arrangement both say they like and in which they have no problems separating business from their personal life.

As for those extraordinarily named players mentioned at the start of the day's play, they had mixed results, so much so that Lourdes Dominguez Lino, a lady, found her name in the men's results section in *The Times*. Not only that, she had the day's most decisive victory 6-0 6-1 over the Italian, Romina Oprandi.

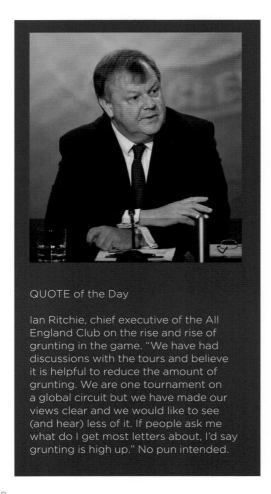

QUOTE of the Day

Ian Ritchie, chief executive of the All England Club on the rise and rise of grunting in the game. "We have had discussions with the tours and believe it is helpful to reduce the amount of grunting. We are one tournament on a global circuit but we have made our views clear and we would like to see (and hear) less of it. If people ask me what do I get most letters about, I'd say grunting is high up." No pun intended.

DAY THREE
22.06.2011

V. Williams
vs
Date-Krumm

Robson
vs
Kerber

Watson
vs
Johansson

Nadal
vs
Sweeting

A. Murray
vs
Kamke

Wawrinka
vs
Bolelli

WEDNESDAY 22ND JUNE...

It was the day that Chelsea FC unveiled their new manager, aged 33 and Wimbledon gave one of its prime appointments to a Japanese player who is still playing singles at 40. For the Blues, it was Andre Villas-Boas; for the green and purples, the star of the show was Kimiko Date-Krumm.

"We like to be attacking and creative and we want to defend in a certain way of how the game should be played, we are very proud of that." That was Villas-Boas talking, not Date-Krumm, but it could well have been the other way around. And Date-Krumm was strutting her stuff in front of a new knight of the realm, Sir Bruce Forsyth who, watching her gentle steps and remarkable stage craft might have tried to sign her up for the next series of *Strictly Come Dancing*.

HRH The Duchess of Cornwall was in the Royal Box as well, marvelling at the sight of someone who gave up the sport once but decided, after a nine year hiatus, that she might come back and give it another crack." I can enjoy to play tennis, maybe I continue to play. I don't know how long I can play any more. Hopefully."

To be precise, the Japanese was 40 years and 267 days old when she stepped onto Centre Court to play Venus Williams, a spring chicken by comparison at 31 years and five days. Date-Krumm is what statisticians call an 'outlier' (and not to mention a testament to the health-giving qualities of sushi and green tea). Her first appearance at Wimbledon came in 1989, which was before 36 members of this year's ladies' draw had even been born.

Kimiko Date-Krumm

Venus Williams

And how wonderful was this about the wonderfully expressive Japanese? As the rain pattered on the roof of Centre Court, she pushed all the way in a three-set sizzler that lasted almost three hours, at which the two players received a standing ovation and the Japanese media fussed and fluttered around me in the press centre asking what I had thought of it all. How could one be anything else but as generous in spirit to their player as she had been to her audience?

Date-Krumm's performance was a combination of the brilliant and the occasionally inept. She hit the ball so flat and low that there is a tiny margin between a scorching winner and a limp larrup into the net. Still, this 'Where Eagles Dare' approach, to use the words of the *Daily Telegraph's* Simon Briggs left Williams in such a lather that, after half an hour, the American was 5-1 down.

Williams responded by powering down serves of up to 120mph but Date-Krumm kept bunting them back with her peculiar pancake forehand, which she hits in such an unassuming style that she might be wielding a frying pan rather than a racket.

"You don't really get a rhythm against her," said a relieved four time champion afterwards. "I have never played anyone who hits the ball like this, or who comes to the net as much as she does." Asked whether Date-Krumm was flying the flag for the more experienced women in tennis, Williams replied "She's a huge role model."

Williams walked on court in the same costume that she wore in the first round: an embroidered romper-suit that appeared to have been constructed from a pair of net curtains. (At least her opponent might have been old enough to recognise the 1970s style reference). But her drapes were drooping by the later stages of the match as Date-Krumm displayed the sort of stamina that a teenager might envy.

The Japanese had already given evidence of her mental strength in the first set, which she took on a tie-break after Williams had saved no fewer than seven set points. The standard might have dropped a little in the second set (Date-Krumm later admitted that her limbs had felt heavy at that stage), but the third was another humdinger.

➤

Laura Robson

And with the roof reflecting back the sound of the crowd's applause, the atmosphere on Centre Court became quite feverish. Date-Krumm had the backing of most of the fans, even if they could not work out what to call her. When she missed her first serve on the big points, a groan came from the Centre Court grandees, who have spent more time watching the Williams sisters over the past decade than they care to remember.

Every time one of the sisters goes out on court, there is some sort of drama. Yesterday Date-Krumm even suggested that Williams had been deliberately throwing up her ball toss and declining to hit it, so as to work out which side of the court her opponent was moving towards, though she described this as "clever tactics" rather than anything underhand. Williams herself explained that her competitive mindset has been her greatest asset since her latest comeback.

At the opposite end of the age range, it had been a squally few months for Laura Robson, a period of consideration, of coming to terms with the process of ageing and growing. At 17, she had just decided to part company with her second professional coach and was re-starting the journey that had begun as a 14-year-old when she won the girls singles in 2008.

How good it was to see her on Court No.16 against Angelique Kerber, of Germany, the world No.77, middling the ball with all that junior verve. There were not many players who strike a ball as sweetly as Robson. The consideration had always been whether she can get into the positions as quickly as required to make that perfect contact. It has been a while since one had seen her play with the measured authority she brought to bear on her fellow left-hander.

In the recent past, Robson had had to idle away the pain of growing into her body while Heather Watson enthralled us with her diligent progress. It is really quite astonishing how, in the space of a couple of hours, Watson should have had one of her lowest days – an elbow injury denying her the prospect of a sustained challenge to Mathilde Johansson of France and which left her in tears in the interview room – and Robson her best for quite some considerable time.

Robson beat Kerber 4-6 7-6 6-3, with an equanimity that was not disturbed when, on the threshold of success, her opponent called for a trainer to massage her shoulder. That was playing fast and loose with the moral code by which tennis ought to be played at this level (nothing was done about it, of course) and so having to wrap herself in at least three club towels to keep out the cold, Robson was forced to ponder the consequences of victory, and defeat.

I had written a couple of days before The Championships that it was vitally important to keep Robson's progress in perspective – she was No.254 in the world when all was said and done. If Virginia Wade, the last British

Wimbledon champion, was coming over all unnecessary in the commentary box, those by the side of the court had to retain a degree of impassive support. It was just so nice to feel the heart beat a little faster watching a home player taking the game to the opposition.

As for Watson, she said she just felt her elbow go, something that had never happened to her before. Why couldn't it have happened at another tournament? Why this one? When it did she was reluctant to hit out and that gave Johansson, who had been restricted at the start, a wave of optimism and she came through 2-6, 6-4, 6-4.

On Centre Court it was another 'roof' day and another occasion to mark the subtle nuances of the court when played open or closed. The Hawk-Eye equipment that had become as much a part of the Wimbledon fabric as the Full English Breakfast in the Media Restaurant, demonstrated that during his match against Ryan Sweeting, the American, Rafael Nadal's serve was 4mph slower on average than it had been against Michael Russell on the opening day.

"Due to the increase in humidity, when the roof is closed, balls are heavier and travel slightly slower through the air," Pete Irwin, one of the Hawk-Eye specialists at the tournament, explained. It was very apt, too, that Rod Sheard, the Australian chief architect of the roof, was also one of the Club's main guests on the day. "It was wonderful to be in there and see so many people enjoying the tennis as the rain lashed down," he said. "We've preserved the character and the intimacy of Centre Court. It doesn't feel like a vast, dominant structure, it's just like the old court, just with an umbrella up."

Nadal could have played for a while with one hand on an umbrella, so dominant was he in his 6-3, 6-2, 6-4 victory over Sweeting, a tall, formidable opponent. According to Simon Barnes in *The Times* "Nadal got down to his usual task of beating tennis balls to death. If he was in a Cluedo set, he'd be the lead piping. Nadal is driven by the belief that if he were ever to let a ball go by without a fight, they would cease to love him, the power would drain from his mighty arms and the bears would get him."

Heather Watson

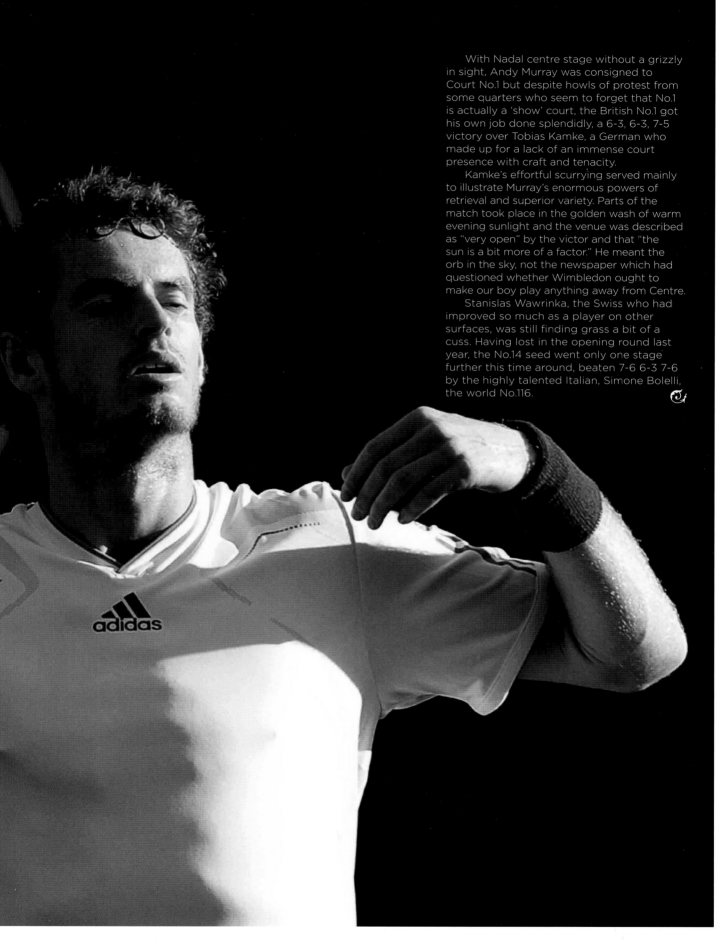

With Nadal centre stage without a grizzly in sight, Andy Murray was consigned to Court No.1 but despite howls of protest from some quarters who seem to forget that No.1 is actually a 'show' court, the British No.1 got his own job done splendidly, a 6-3, 6-3, 7-5 victory over Tobias Kamke, a German who made up for a lack of an immense court presence with craft and tenacity.

Kamke's effortful scurrying served mainly to illustrate Murray's enormous powers of retrieval and superior variety. Parts of the match took place in the golden wash of warm evening sunlight and the venue was described as "very open" by the victor and that "the sun is a bit more of a factor." He meant the orb in the sky, not the newspaper which had questioned whether Wimbledon ought to make our boy play anything away from Centre.

Stanislas Wawrinka, the Swiss who had improved so much as a player on other surfaces, was still finding grass a bit of a cuss. Having lost in the opening round last year, the No.14 seed went only one stage further this time around, beaten 7-6 6-3 7-6 by the highly talented Italian, Simone Bolelli, the world No.116.

DAY FOUR
23.06.2011

Djokovic
vs
Anderson

S. Williams
vs
Halep

Lisicki
vs
Li Na

Tsonga
vs
Dimitrov

Soderling
vs
Hewitt

J. Murray and
Stakhovsky
vs
Rice and Thornley

THURSDAY 23RD JUNE...

The photograph had been posted on his Twitter page, from the back garden of his home which was an errant lob's distance away from the Club. Every morning, a local squirrel (I say local but it could have popped over from Tooting for all we knew) came and perched on the table in the back of Novak Djokovic's rented accommodation. He couldn't resist taking a picture of it.

"She's getting closer and closer each day so maybe by the end of the fortnight I'll have her eating out of my hand," Djokovic said. Might it have been a portentous few words given his desire to land the coveted title? We would have to wait and see.

As for the routine of placing one foot in front of another and getting the job of reaching the second week of The Championships, Djokovic was going about it all the right way, a 6-3 6-4 6-2 victory over South African, Kevin Anderson, being completed in five minutes shy of two hours. He could be back striking the squirrel's chin before nightfall.

Watching his demolition of Anderson, one was struck once more by the levels of finesse and fitness that had been the hallmark of Djokovic's astonishing progress throughout the tennis world in the past six months. Belief had replaced benign resistance, mentally honed, physical pitch perfect, he looked like the perfect tennis specimen and it worried the rest of the pack. At one stage he produced a splits shot every bit as phenomenal as anything Kim Clijsters had ever attempted

James Lawton, of the *Independent*, who had studied athletes at close quarter for many years, recognised the newness in Djokovic. "The eruption (against Anderson) came early in the second set of three which saw him at times not only come close to dismembering his giant opponent but also announce a state of mind so exuberant, so hungry for new glory that no one, not (Roger) Federer, not the overwhelming favourite Rafael Nadal and certainly not Andy Murray could begin to ignore it.

"Djokovic repelled three crashing attempted winners from Anderson before beating him with a return of stunning power and placement. The crowd observed a millisecond of silence, then shrieked. Djokovic? He simply flew into the air suspended, literally by the force of his belief that his greatest triumph – a Wimbledon title to add to his two Australian Opens – may now just be over a week away."

Djokovic, who had now lost only one of his 44 matches in the year, had not even had a second thought about being asked to play his second round match on Court No.1. For Serena Williams, playing only her fourth match of 2011, the sense of disappointment at having to play on Court No.2 against Simona Halep, of Romania, was clear.

Novak Djokovic

Williams had cried after winning her first-round match on Centre Court. There were no tears this time but there were squeals of imprecation and shrieks of irritation. The defending champion struggled badly at the start, losing the first set which stung her into life and the American won 3-6, 6-2, 6-1. But in the beginning she was playing so far below her best that it seemed likely she was heading for elimination.

Williams's father, Richard, said that he felt his daughter was playing at about "49% to 50% of her best", and that felt about right. "She still has all that power," Richard said. "She's just not using it at the right time."

In the first set Williams was bamboozled by Halep's serve, such that her returns were either shanked sideways or ballooned back over the net. Halep, who is 19 and ranked No. 57 in the world, played a dogged baseline game, full of gritty endeavour. She broke in the fourth game and held on to take the first set, to the evident annoyance of Williams, who started to slap her thighs and berate herself under her breath between points.

Her father said that, after surgery to remove a blood clot in her lungs "she was so close to dying that whether she ever wins again or loses every match she plays, I'm just thanking God that she is alive." One surmised Serena did not feel quite the same way. She has a champion's pride and was furious she was making so many mistakes. "I feel like I'm in shape," she said, "but I'm playing my way into match condition."

Williams broke Halep early in the second set and from that point she wrested control away from her opponent. Halep slipped three times and had to call on her trainer to treat her left knee after she twisted it. She did not play nearly so well afterwards.

Williams found some semblance of form in the second set and turned the third into

Simona Halep

Serena Williams

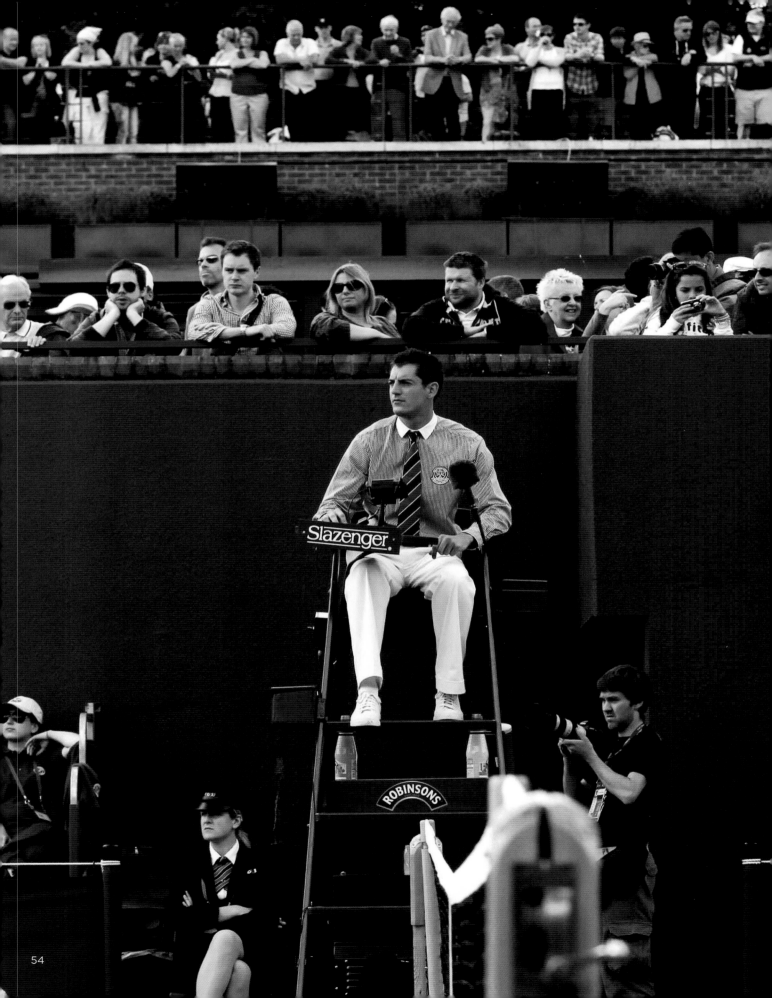

something of a procession. She had three match points and was 5-0 up when she let her concentration slip and lost the next seven points. When the win finally came it was accompanied by a scream of satisfaction.

The same was true of Sabine Lisicki, though in different surroundings and at a different place in her career. Lisicki, the German, had been the recipient of a wild card into the Championships, having won the AEGON Classic in Edgbaston a week before the tournament began and for her bravery in the face of an ankle injury the extent of which was that she said she had to learn how to walk properly again.

She beat Li Na, 3-6 6-4 8-6, prompting the *Daily Mirror* to suggest that it was the finest Chinese takeaway in Wimbledon history. "They don't need towels at Wimbledon any more," wrote Christopher Clarey, of the *New York Times*. "They require handkerchiefs." That line was in response to Lisicki showing the full range of her emotions after victory over Li Na, a couple of days after Serena's sobs filled the air.

In 2009 at Wimbledon, Lisicki looked set to become a major factor when she reached the quarter-finals at the age of 19, but serious injury forced her to miss five months of last season. She won only five matches all year and nearly dropped out of the top 200. But after rehabilitating her ankle and switching to a gluten-free diet (exactly like Novak Djokovic), Lisicki is back in rare form on the grass.

On another rainy day which prompted the closing of the Centre Court roof, the German generated the biggest thunderclap of the tournament by saving two match points against third-seeded Chinese star who had just won the French Open and yet had long said she preferred grass to red clay. One can now presume that the 116 million Chinese who watched Li triumph at Roland Garros will find other programming during the Wimbledon women's final.

Sabine Lisicki (left) and Li Na

"I didn't feel different, I didn't feel, like, pressure," Li said of her new status. "The only change is right now opponents see you different. So everyone play against you, they feeling, 'Nothing to lose.' So they can play best tennis on the court. I don't think this player (Lisicki) can stay same level like today. If like this, I mean she's No.1 in the world."

Li Na's coach, Michael Mortensen, the Dane, concurred. "Sabine is serving like most of the men are serving," he said. Lisicki slammed 17 aces saving her most powerful display for when she needed it most. Down by 3-5, 15-40 in the final set, she saved the two match points with service winners and closed out the game with consecutive aces up the middle. Her first serves on those critical points were 122, 123, 124 and 122 miles an hour. All four serves were faster than any other woman has hit at Wimbledon this year, including Venus and Serena Williams.

Jo-Wilfried Tsonga's 'post-match dance routine'

Tsonga consoles Grigor Dimitrov after their match

"I always had that powerful serve, and I think it's one of the best in women's tennis," said Lisicki, who is tall at 5 feet 10 inches, with powerful legs that help her generate that pace out of her knee bend.

The match of the day was clearly that between Jo-Wilfried Tsonga, the beaten finalist at Queen's 11 days earlier and the young Bulgarian, Grigor Dimitrov, the 2008 boys' champion at the Club. Tsonga won if 6-7 6-4 6-4 7-6 and, at the end of the match, with Dimitrov flat on his front, Tsonga came over to his opponent's side to pick him up, hug him and then set off on his usual post-match dance routine.

"He was a bit on fire sometimes," Tsonga said of the teenager. "I thought if I stayed consistent he would miss but he didn't miss and it was a very difficult match. I am very happy to get through." Dimitrov's was a story of how exciting things can happen to a player when young but that they have to retain that focus, seek to improve, never rest on their laurels.

On the back of his success three years earlier, Dimitrov broke into the world's top 300 but a nasty injury at Wimbledon a year later stopped his momentum. Twelve months ago he was down to No.342 and

Robin Soderling

Lleyton Hewitt

treading water. He joined forces with Peter McNamara, through the Patrick Mouratoglou academy, outside Paris. The Bulgarian and the Australian – a man who won three Grand Slam doubles titles – hit it off immediately. He began the tournament ranked 62, is heading for the top 50 and much higher.

Dimitrov was, at the time of The Championships, the youngest player in the top 100 and Peter Lundgren, the Swede who coached both Dimitrov and Roger Federer, once said the Bulgarian was the better of the two when they were 18 and now his game was beginning to take shape, with his superb athleticism matched by outstanding shot-making.

The No.5 seed in the men's game survived an enormous scare against a former champion but had the muscle and the intent to survive. Robin Soderling who says he plays tennis to be the best in the world, was on the receiving end of a hammering from Lleyton Hewitt, the Australian who had been there. Hewitt was a Wimbledon champion, too, in 2002 and in front of his raucous fans started with a reminder of what had taken him to both glories.

Hewitt played spectacular tennis for two set but Soderling gradually wore him down, winning 6-7 3-6 7-5 6-4 6-4. "I love competing and I especially love competing in this event," said the father of three, who may be preparing to spend rather more time with his offspring. "As long as my body is close to 100 per cent, I want to go out there and compete."

In the doubles, there was a bit of a rude awakening for Sergiy Stakhovsky, the player from Ukraine who had teamed up with Jamie Murray in the men's event. Stakhovsky needed ice treatment to his right ear after Jamie's wayward serve caught his mate flush on the side of the face. "I'd been serving really well all match and then I threw the ball up, it took a bit of a gust of wind, I tried to fight it but it hit Sergiy right in the ear, which wasn't ideal." After a rub down with the ice, Stakhovsky was able to continue and the combination defeated the British pair, David Rice and Sean Thornley, 6-3 7-5 to reach the second round.

DAY FIVE
24.06.2011

A. Murray
vs
Ljubicic
___

Robson
vs
Sharapova
___

Baltacha
vs
Peng
___

Roddick
vs
Lopez
___

Tomic
vs
Andreev
___

Ivan Ljubicic

FRIDAY 24TH JUNE...

Ron Weasley took a day off from Hogwarts to attend Wimbledon – and there was plenty of Expelliarmus on the Centre Court, just for his pleasure. Some Wingardium Leviosa too. Much of this was courtesy of Andy Murray, who occasionally played like a bit of a wizard himself.

The actor, Rupert Grint, who was wearing seriously large dark sunglasses despite the fact that the roof was closed for most of the day, came and saw for himself that there is another prince of darkness to add to the list of those with whom he has regularly crossed celluloid swords. Murray, the British No.1, defeated Croatia's Ivan Ljubicic, who looks as if he could be a character out of Harry Potter with his shiny skull and throbbing cranial veins, 6-4 4-6 6-1 7-6 to take his place in the fourth round.

Ljubicic, at 32, was the oldest player to reach the last 32 and was the oldest ever first-time winner of an ATP Tour when he won the

BNP Paribas Masters in Indian Wells, California last year, a sure sign of getting better as he got balder. He arrived at Wimbledon, an event where he did not have a good record, with a thumping great serve and a natty one-handed backhand. Murray came with his talent and his ambition, and occasionally found the two working in opposition.

For Ljubicic, this was a new experience on two counts – a first visit to grass court tennis under lights and a debut on Centre in his 12th visit to the tournament. Given the higher quality of the opponent, this was a significant step up for Murray, especially given that there were passages of play when Ljubicic knocked Murray out of his rhythm, others when the Scot was at his sumptuous best.

The weather was said to be warming up the following week and few people would be more delighted with that than Murray for ➤

whom the novelty of the roof appeared to be wearing off. Three times he had played beneath it now and none had been very comfortable but he did survive a full on assault from Ljubicic and, once again, he was confident to play his special 'hot-dog shot', which may have had another name in Hogwarts-speak. "Plucking a half volley from between his legs and dropping it over the net like a snowflake," was the description of Mike Dickson, in the *Daily Mail*.

"I was in just the right position," Murray remarked, a little shyly, of his showpiece. "I tried it (and it worked) at Queen's a couple of weeks ago and also in practice and I haven't missed one yet. I'd look like a plonker if I did."

While Andy was weaving his little pieces of Potter magic, there were traces of spellbinding tennis from Laura 'Hermione' Robson on Court No.1 and it was not as though she did not give Maria Sharapova, a former champion, a bit of a scare. Initially, indeed, it looked as if she had the Russian under some kind of spell.

Apparently, Laura had not been on her finest behaviour the week before the event to the extent that Kathy, her mother and coach again had confiscated her rackets, locked them in the back of the car and told her daughter to buck her ideas up if she wanted to be a proper professional.

All we saw against Sharapova was thorough professionalism, a level of performance that raised local pulses and made the Russian realise that, unless she played at somewhere approaching a very decent level, she could be out on her ear, dangly earrings and all.

In her ninth consecutive Wimbledon appearance at the age of 24, eventually she won 7-6 6-3 and if the levels of noise she emitted in the process of hitting her strokes was now seriously a matter for the authorities — how can it not be an interference to her opponent? — the edge of experience was fundamental.

As for Robson, she played more decent shots in four hours of tennis here than in the

Maria Sharapova

past year and for that there was a genuine sense of consolation. Her problems in recent months with hip troubles and stomach muscle tears, combined with a sudden spurt in height made keeping her in a positive spirit as important as anything else.

It was only a couple of weeks before Wimbledon that she played her first WTA Tour-level event of the year — and the eighth of her career, to give her period away some perspective — and lost in a grass-court event in 's-Hertogenbosch, in the Netherlands, after which she promptly decided to change the people around her.

Patrick Mouratoglou, a Frenchman who had chosen to take some time away from his academy in Paris to coach Robson full-time, was informed that she would be going back to work, ostensibly with Kathy, who would now look to piece together a team who could succour and shield Robson on the next stage of her development.

Robson's game had always been easy on the eye. Being a left-hander undoubtedly helped. It was such a boon to have a serve of considerable pep that could sweep away to a right-hander's backhand in the advantage court — just ask Andy Roddick after Feliciano López zoned in on that corner on Centre Court to such effect on the same day (of which more later). More than that, Robson had a court presence; always had had.

It helped to walk on, especially against someone who held her head as high as Sharapova, with an equally upright and "look the world right in the eye" attitude. Surviving five break points in her first service game did not do much for her nerves but every time she was down, Robson's response was full of positive intent. So much so that from the second deuce in her first service game, the world No.6 promptly served two double faults and was 2-0 down, which became 3-0. The patrons of Court No.1 were becoming decidedly giddy.

Perhaps Robson's greatest opportunity arrived in the sixth game, leading 4-1, when Sharapova did not make a single first serve, but neither did the teenager offer enough of a threat on her return. The tiny squeals of disappointment were as nothing compared with the haunting noises made by Sharapova as she broke back — two double faults did not aid the British cause — and if she made a hash of every challenge she attempted in the first set, the Russian's levels were raised sufficiently in the tie-break.

Sharapova dashed into a 5-1 lead in the second, but Robson's game response was more in the way of encouragement. "I thought it was a world-class performance," Kathy said of her daughter, and the fact that in the previous 37 matches she had played on these grounds only seven players had gathered more games against Sharapova than Robson bore out that comment.

"Keep learning, keep playing and keep working hard," were the nuggets of advice offered from a one-time 17-year-old Grand Slam champion to a 17-year-old who yearns for such success one day. Neither, in her day, did Sharapova have the limitations placed on her ability to play as many matches as she wanted that are now rigorously enforced by the WTA's age eligibility rules.

Laura Robson

Above: Elena Baltacha and Shuai Peng (below)

"What it really comes to is grinding it out in the matches when you don't necessarily have thousands of people behind you. You're in the third set and you have to win those matches because it ultimately leads to experience," Sharapova said.

Elena Baltacha, the British No.1 may also have heeded those words for she was engaged in a palpitation-inducing three-setter on Court No.18 against Shuai Peng of China, another gritty little performer from that nation. Baltacha won the first set, dropped the second and began to look, to most observers, as if she was over-emotional, and less consistent. She broke in the first game, was broken back, led 4-2 and even saved three match points but all the while there was a feeling in the pit on one's stomach that it may not work out for her. "I'm playing the best I've played in my whole career but I haven't peaked yet," the 27-year-old said.

As for Roddick, three-times the runner-up and never the champion, was out-aced 28 to 23, out-passed and simply outplayed by Lopez. He admitted he had not played well for more than a year now but, ever the optimist, he believed things could get better. "I don't think I've played my best since probably April of last year," Roddick said. "I think I can improve. Have I over the last year? Probably not. I've been up against some stuff. But it has to get better, there's no doubt."

Roddick had won all seven of his previous meetings with López, now ranked 44 but who has been inside the top 20. The left-hander was one of the streakier players in the game around but when it all gelled (which was not reflection on his hair which never seemed to have a strand out of place), he was world class. López played two superb tie-breaks to take command and then an early break in the

third set was enough to seal victory and a fourth-round place.

"I have probably played like **** in third round matches and won before," Roddick said. "The thing you guys have to understand is there's no script. Some days you're going to play well and lose and some days you're going to play like **** and win. What do you do? You keep moving forward until you decide to stop. At this point I've not decided to stop so I'll keep moving forward."

Rafael Nadal was allowed only one set against Gilles Muller, of Luxembourg, and that was a bit of a strain, before the rains interrupted. How deeply Muller may have lived to regret the smash he totally cooked while a mini-break ahead in the tie-break into which he had so assiduously fought was a moot point. Probably at least as deeply as he might come to regret the double fault he served at

Andy Roddick

6-6, allowing Nadal, who had begun to pace the back of the court with greater concern than usual, to serve out for the set and ease the growing palpitations of his faithful.

On the outer courts there was a sizeably impressive win for the young Australian, Bernard Tomic, who defeated Igor Andreev, of Russia, from two sets down, 4-6 5-7 6-3 6-4 6-1, gradually running a very competent performer into the ground. We had been waiting for Tomic to build on his tremendous junior record and a win like this one would serve to assuage Australian hopes after the previous day's defeat of Lleyton Hewitt, whom the young man was hoping to emulate one day.

When you saw Tomic at work, you could begin to believe in wizardry.

QUOTE of the Day

Ryan Harrison, the rookie American lucky loser, extended David Ferrer, the No.7 seed to five sets before losing 6-7 6-1 4-6 6-3 6-2.

"Talking about David, he brings the same focus and attention to every single point, whereas I've checked out a couple of times. I don't lose concentration or physically lose effort but it's a matter of making sure that every single point you play is thought out, with a purpose. Sometimes you can just get caught in thinking about the situation and what might happen after the match, which is irrelevant to the process of winning."

DAY SIX
25.06.2011

Djokovic
vs
Baghdatis

Nadal
vs
Muller

Federer
vs
Nalbandian

Fish
vs
Haase

S Williams
vs
Kirilenko

Tomic
vs
Soderling

Monfils
vs
Kubot

Ivanovic
vs
Cetkovska

Schiavone
vs
Paszek

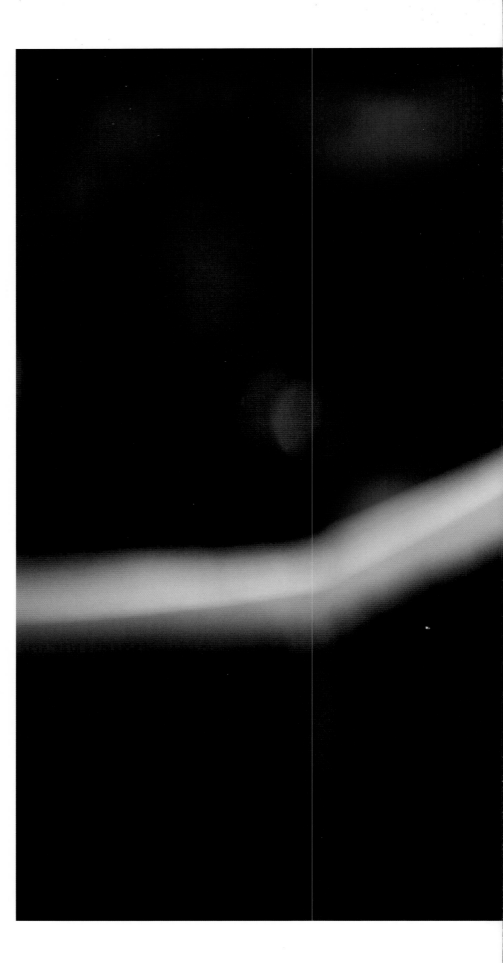

SATURDAY 25TH JUNE...

Armed Forces Day was celebrated with gusto on Centre Court with privileged seats in a prominent section of the Royal Box given to those brave souls from the Army, Navy and Royal Air Force who do the real work while we lucky few gallivant around the world watching tennis. What a rousing reception they received from the crowd, a deserved recognition of the pride in them that never fades.

Rubbing shoulders with our troops were those from the world of sport who have set a gold standard of performance, the like of which makes knights and dames of them and is a reminder that while we may have struggled to produce champions in tennis for a few years, our success in other pastimes remains daunting.

From Sir Steve Redgrave, to Dame Kelly Holmes, from Sir Geoff Hurst (my particular hero, 1966 and all that) to rugby stalwarts, all were here to celebrate the half way mark in The Championships, and the best was saved until the last there, as Marcos Baghdatis and Novak Djokovic engaged in a four set struggle which set the tone. The talk had been so much of the top four at the event that those on the undercard had become a touch demeaned by it.

Baghdatis was a former Australian Open runner-up, he once had to play a match Down Under against Lleyton Hewitt that lasted until 4.30 in the morning (why couldn't they have built Melbourne Park in a residential area so they had to close down by 11 at the latest!), had been a quarter-finalist at The Championships and was one of those players who always wore his heart on his sleeve. Because of all of this, the fact he was a bit of a radical and still people in Britain weren't quite sure of Djokovic, the crowd seemed to be leaning towards the Cypriot's side.

Perhaps that was a touch unfair on Djokovic but what unfolded was a match of such abandon, fruitful tennis, pulsating changes of pace and impetus that everyone was sated. The gremlins could get to the new world No.2 as well though. It was a close run thing which was harder for the Serbian to deal with – Baghdatis, who was at his coruscating finest at times - or his inner demons, as Simon Cambers correctly opined in the *Observer*.

One smashed up racket told the story after a beautiful rally at 4-3, 30-all in the second set, when he missed a routine backhand, Djokovic did not just take one divot from the surface in front of the assembled troops, but three of them. Eddie Seaward, the head groundsman, would not have been too delighted at that. "It was frustrating, I cannot lie," Djokovic said. "I did lose my temper, I didn't feel great on the court. My legs weren't working. You have those days." He won the match though, 6-4 4-6 6-3 6-4, so that was a heartener.

Novak Djokovic

Marcos Baghdatis

With Djokovic earning his place in the last 16, he was joined by Rafael Nadal who returned from the postponement of play on Friday evening to complete a 7-6 7-6 6-0 victory over the big man from Luxembourg, Gilles Muller. It did seem as though the big four was moving inexorably towards the same showdown that had been enjoyed at the French Open a month earlier.

The last time we had witnessed such a convergence of male talent in the game, was when Pete Sampras and Andre Agassi regularly crossed swords before Federer became the squire of Centre Court. "The only thing I can say is that before, in my opinion, the top four didn't play as solidly (consistently) as they do today," Nadal said.

"Probably in the past that didn't happen a lot," the Spaniard added. "The courts were a little bit slower today and that means the best have a little more chance to play the points and if you have the more time to play the points, the best players have the best chances to win."

Roger Federer was also into the last 16, courtesy of a routine victory over Argentina's David Nalbandian who simply did not have the manoueverablity to beat someone of the Swiss man's talents these days. It was good to see Nalbandian back on Centre but he did not really test Federer as a player should be tested at this stage of a major.

"I'm very happy if I keep playing this way," Federer said after winning 6-4 6-2 6-4 in one hour and 46 minutes on Centre Court, his home for so many years. "It's a matter of keeping it up and then adjusting to what's coming from opponents. They all play very differently." This was a victory in the classic mould, embroidered with precision and elegance, and it reminded peers, doubters and mischief-makers that there is enough life in his 29-year-old Swiss legs to carry him a little further yet.

The world No.3, caught in an A3-like traffic jam behind Nadal and Djokovic for several months, affects to not caring about passing Pete Sampras' record of seven Wimbledon titles (half of the American's total haul). Believe that if you like.

Wimbledon and its grass surface would also seem a match made in heaven for Mardy Fish, the American who possesses a big serve and a varied assortment of shots including a backhand slice that skids and stays low. He was also at home at the net, a throwback who described moving forward after a serve to put away a volley as "a kind of rush, like hitting a home run in baseball."

Against Robin Haase, the elegant Dutchman, Fish ventured to the net 53 times and won 41 of those points. He also earned 20 break points — including seven in one 28-point game in the second set — three of which he converted. "It's one of those things

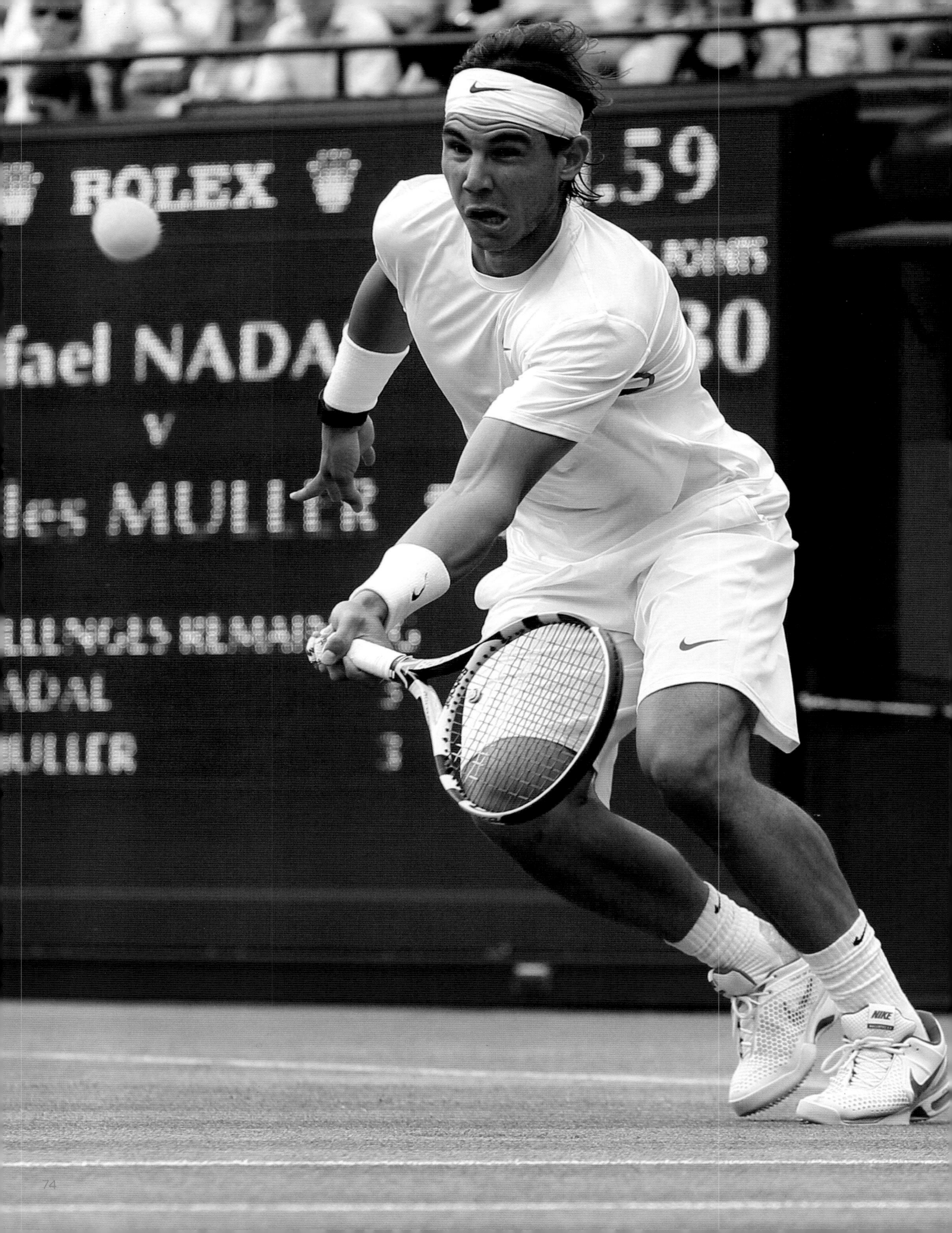
ROLEX

where you keep throwing darts at a wall and eventually something's going to stick," he added, adding to his sporting analogies.

Fish's direction and timings had been maddeningly off at Wimbledon before now. Despite his comfort on the surface, he had not been beyond the third round in eight previous appearances, which was a concern. Last year, he came to The Championships fresh from a runners-up appearance at Queen's then felt stale. This time, he was beaten in the third round in Paris and decided that Stacy, his wife, and Charlie, his newly-acquired dachshund, needed him more. "I think this time last year I was spent," he said. "I was eight weeks into a trip and that was no good for me."

Speaking of Americans on journeys, Serena Williams appeared to be back in her groove. Giggling her way through the post-match press conference following her first straight-sets win of the tournament – against the No.26 seed Maria Kirilenko of Russia – the four-time champion was in a buoyant mood.

It was all in stark contrast to her anger and affront days earlier over the issue of being made to play on Court No.2. But against Kirilenko she was back in grander surroundings and was prepared to forget the controversy, only adding: "I think yesterday (Friday) we saw three women's matches on the show courts, which was the first time. It's always good to see three women's and three men's matches. You know, it is what it is," she said. ➤

Mardy Fish

There was a renewed sparkle around the No.7 seed. She practically beamed when asked if she agreed with bookmakers establishing her as one of the favourites to win the title for a fifth time. "Um, I wouldn't bet against me," she said and it did look as if she had a point. Having dropped a set in each of her first two matches, the 29-year-old swiftly dispatched Kirilenko – despite the Russian posing a few problems along the way – winning 6-3 6-2.

After the traumas of last year – falling off her bike, as one journalist put it to her – had she finally found her pedals again? The metaphor turned literal as, burying her head on the table in front of her in an attempt to control her giggles, Williams revealed that she had, in fact, fallen off her bike last October leaving a permanent scar on her right shoulder. "It was a pink Beach Cruiser," she said. "I was riding in my community (in Florida) and I wasn't obeying local traffic laws. I was going too fast. I just couldn't control the speed and I fell. It was horrible."

The same way as Robin Soderling felt horrible for much of the day. The big Swede, facing Bernard Tomic of Australia on Court No.1, was not himself, he was falling to his haunches after most rallies, he needed on-court attention during changeovers and he could not contend not at all with the varieties of spin and slice that are are fulcrums of Tomic's play.

The first set went by in 17 minutes and if Soderling looked dizzy, it was only understandable. The Swede motioned, or semi-motioned, to his coaches' box but there was little they could do to staunch the flow of Australian winners and Swedish lurches. Tomic won 6-1 6-4 7-5 to become the youngest male to reach the fourth round at The Championships since Michael Chang of the United States, 21 years earlier. Not only that, he had accumulated enough ranking points to become Australia's No.1 player for the first time.

Soderling was not the only player from the top 10 seeds to fall as Gael Monfils, the Frenchman, who was once the junior champion, fell with not a great deal of grace or steadfastness to Lucasz Kubot, the Polish qualifier 6-3 3-6 6-3 6-3. It was to be the signal for the parting of the ways between Monfils and Roger Rasheed, the Australian who had coached him for the past three years from No.40 in the world into the highest echelon.

➤

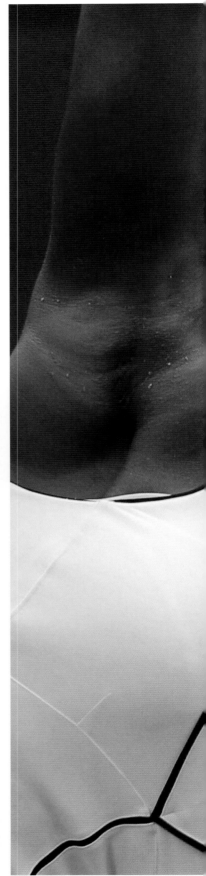

There were to be changes too in the coaching set up of Ana Ivanovic, after the former world No.1 fell to the world No.81, Petra Cetkovska, from the Czech Republic. Ivanovic, still only 23, had wanted to appoint Nigel Sears, who was head coach of women's tennis at the LTA to travel with her full time for a couple of years; Sears had initially resisted but now he believed the time had come to change direction. We would have to wait and see what kind of impact it would have on the development of British players, for whom Sears had been largely responsible for over four years.

In the second best women's match of the tournament, to far, the No.9 seed, Francesca Schiavone, of Italy, was defeated 3-6, 6-4, 11-9 by Tamira Paszek, the Austrian who, when she had had to qualify for the tournament three years ago, actually rented a room in the nearby home of Mike Dickson, the *Daily Mail* tennis correspondent. Suffice it to say, he was pretty happy about the result.

DAY SEVEN
27.06.2011

S. Williams
vs
Bartoli

V. Williams
vs
Pironkova

A. Murray
vs
Gasquet

Nadal
vs
Del Potro

Lopez
vs
Kubot

Wozniacki
vs
Cibulkova

Federer
vs
Youzhny

Tsonga
vs
Ferrer

MONDAY 27TH JUNE...

Of course, Sunday had been beautiful, not a cloud in the sky, sunscreen required, what did one expect? A day spent watching players come and go to practice, a bit of meet and greet, a hint of nerves here, a few jaws grimly set, the knowledge that the following day would bring revelation and rejoicing to some, sombre moods and sadness among others.

It was that special day in the tennis calendar, the second Monday, fourth round day, there would be 16 singles matches that would be bound to test everyone's mettle, players, writers, broadcasters, supporters and staff alike for there was nowhere in the world where so much happened on one tennis day. And, to top it all off, the Club announced they were expecting a couple of rather special visitors.

Fortunately, though, the edge had been knocked a bit off the temperature, the morning arrived every bit as calm and welcoming as had been the day of rest (for some). Who would have guessed, as we made our way back into the grounds, that by the end of play, one world No.1 would be out, the other would look as if he was on his way, the sisters had packed their bags, we would have our youngest male quarter-finalist in a quarter of a century, Andy Murray would romp home before apologising to the Duke and Duchess of Cambridge for "being a bit sweaty" and another British player had taken the first step on what looked like an encouraging journey deep into The Championships?

As ever – where to start? Perhaps the most unlikely thud, or make that pair of thuds, landed within an hour and 40 minutes of each other as first Serena and then Venus Williams – with nine Wimbledon singles titles between them in – were dispatched from the tournament. Serena was beaten 6-3 7-6 by Marion Bartoli, of France, her earliest exit since 2005 and Venus was even more heavily thumped, 6-2 6-3 by Tsvetana Pironkova, of Bulgaria, for the second time in consecutive years in SW19. These were ground-shifting

Serena Williams and (below) Marion Bartoli

setbacks. The Sinking Sisterhood, one American publication described it.

Bartoli deserved her victory, no doubt about it, and she had become a legitimate challenger. Remember, of course, four years previously she stunned Justine Henin, then world No.1, before losing to Venus in the final.

Right: Venus Williams

Below: Tsvetana Pironkova

Bartoli had recently reached the last four at Roland Garros, and managed to overcome illness in the previous round. In the process, she notoriously ordered her parents from the stands, but was full of decorous apologies after they cheered her on, the only occupants on her side of the players' box on No.1.

It was gruelling even to watch. "A smothering, flat glare fell upon the court", wrote Chris McGrath in the *Independent*. "Serena completed the warm-up in a cardigan, but was mistaken if she imagined that her opponent might be intimidated by this show of cool. For her own part, Bartoli appeared to be having grievous difficulty in keeping warm. She could not keep still for a moment. Between points, she displayed a fascinating and extensive collection of tics and rituals". We had all seen those before.

By contrast to this French cat on a hot tin roof, Williams introduced the menace of a panther to her slow, easy movement between points. She professed immunity to the curious behaviour of her opponent afterwards. "I really focus on me out there," she said. "I rarely see my opponent. Often I look up and wonder, look at the score to see who I'm playing". Oh really?

But Bartoli was making rather more forcible claims on her attention. In a nutshell, her game-plan appeared to be run hard – and hit harder. She chased every ball down, both hands welded to the racket, and banished it as though it offended her. Whenever Serena missed a first serve, Bartoli would march head ➤

The Duke and Duchess of Cambridge applaud Andy Murray

down across the baseline to prepare for the next. This was no nonsense tennis.

Roars of "Allez" filled the air, the crowd was right on her side, and though Serena fought a champion's fight, she could not withstand the unremitting quality of the French girl's play. She did falter when serving for the match at 6-5 in the second set, leading 40-15. Williams saved three match points before breaking, then another in the tie-break to bring that level at 6-all. A lesser player may have taken the hint but Bartoli kept swinging away, nailing a backhand return into the corner that Williams could only net. It was a fifth match point and, after a practice swing and leap into the air, she delivered her first flat serve down the T. Though Williams touched it with her frame, no string was touched.

"She played well," Williams said of Bartoli. "She should always play like this and would be top five, minimum. It's like 'wow, where is this player through the rest of the year?'" Funny, because that is what everyone else was saying about her.

Venus's exit was altogether more routine and perhaps, therefore, more troubling. Pironkova was the player who had faded when she won the first five games of Serena's comeback match in Eastbourne but there was to be no such letting go of the throat of her elder sister, Venus crumbling in the face of an onslaught of winners. "I think we both envisioned seeing today a little bit different," was Venus's response. And as the sisters were not playing doubles this year, that was their cue to make for the airport.

By the time Venus had appeared on Centre, their Royal Highnesses the Duke and Duchess of Cambridge were meeting Britain's top tennis player behind the closed doors of Centre Court. Their radiances had accepted an invitation to attend, something that was kept a state secret. Perhaps senior

Richard Gasquet

members of the Royal Family should be there every time Murray played for a year ago, Her Majesty the Queen's visit inspired him to a straight set victory over Jarkko Nieminen, the Finn, and this time around, he spanked Richard Gasquet, the Frenchman, 7-6 6-3 6-2, and did not appear in the slightest bit troubled.

"Neither Prince William nor Andy Murray would be called a king just yet," wrote Simon Barnes in *The Times* "but they are both, you might say, nicely placed. You might get better odds on one than you do on the other but both are closer to the possibility than they have ever been before."

If Gasquet's much praised single-handed backhand was frequently on display, so was Murray's two-fisted technique, less elegant but hit flatter with changes of pace that provided a constant challenge to his opponent. Both players suffered in the first set tie-break, each twice capturing the other man's serve before Murray struck the vital blow, ending a long exchange of backhands by switching the angle and forcing a forehand error from the No.17 seed. Two points later the Scot took the set with a rare venture to the net.

His most crucial incision came in the eighth game of the second set, with the first break of serve of the match, after the players had been on court for 93 minutes. He reached break point with a magnificent cross-court backhand, forcing a scurrying Gasquet into an overhit backhand, before serving out for a two-set lead. The third set was little short of a formality. Then, having bowed to the royal couple, Murray was taken to meet them.

"If I'd have known they were coming, I'd have shaved this morning," he said.

Close shaves would become a rage later in the day. When the left ankle of Rafael Nadal, the No.1 seed, was being examined before the first set tie break of his drama-laden victory over Juan Martin Del Potro, of Argentina, deep into the evening, there was a look in the Spaniard's eyes you did not see often. It was of a forlorn, almost fearful man.

Nothing exemplified the spirit of the defending champion more than an insatiable desire to play the game he loves and when the trainer whispered the word 'unusual' into his ear and the tournament doctor was peeling back the wrapping from a packet of pills, it looked for all the world as if Nadal might have to stop. That would have been a desperate pity – for all but Del Potro.

He had turned his left ankle, we could all see that. Once more, Nadal's limbs seemed to be the mercy of his uncompromising attitude. Having gone off for treatment before the tie-break, he then came through it and though the big swinging Del Potro battled back into contention, Nadal held sway against some monstrous hitting, especially on the forehand, and did not look in too much lingering discomfort as he held on for a 7-6 3-6 7-6 6-4 victory and a place in the quarter-finals against Mardy Fish, of the United States.

Murray's opponent would be Feliciano Lopez of Spain who, quite rightly, said that he had been trying out the grass and finding it to his favour long before the current legions of Spanish players arrived. Now 29, Lopez had performed miraculously to recover from two sets down to defeat Lucasz Kubot, a Polish qualifier with a mighty serve and destructive forehand (where hadn't we heard that before) 3-6 6-7 7-6 7-5 7-5, this coming in his 38th consecutive Grand Slam tournament which said much for his physical shape.

This was Caroline Wozniacki's 18th by comparison and she was still searching for that one of unstoppable momentum. Once more, on the grass, it didn't work out for the present No.1 player as the 20-year-old was beaten 1-6 7-6 7-5 by Dominika Cibulkova of Slovakia.

"I cannot really do anything now," Wozniacki said with an air of unremitting gloom as questions about her Grand Slam fallibility, especially after her third-round defeat at Roland Garros, were raised again. "I did my best and it wasn't good enough. I just need to look forward and go back on the practice court."

Her conqueror sounded sympathetic about Wozniacki's plight but there was not much to be seen on Court No.2 where both blazing sun and the Slovak's blazing forehands buried the Dane's ambitions.

Juan Martin Del Potro

Dominika Cibulkova

Caroline Wozniacki

Wozniacki denied that she had been affected by the suffocating heat but she did seem to suffer when trying vainly to chase down the Slovakian's 30 magnificent forehand winners.

Cibulkova, at 5ft 3in, hit with preposterous power. "All or nothing," was how she described her approach with that blitzing forehand, whereas with Wozniacki it just looked too much like a case of safety-first mechanics. She possessed no great weapon but relied instead on wearing down the opposition with a combination of consistency, huge reserves of fitness, patience and defensive resilience. The lesson for Wozniacki, in those final crucial exchanges, ought to be that she was beaten by daring and ambition.

Oh, and Roger Federer dropped his first set of the tournament to Mikhail Youzhny, the Russian before winning 6-7 6-3 6-3 6-3 which probably gave those in his section the idea of attacking him with a little more impression. That would, surely, be the case in the shape of Jo-Wilfried Tsonga, the Frenchman, who swallowed up David Ferrer, the No.7 seed in straight sets, conserving enough energy to have a real go at the Swiss in the quarter-finals.

In the first round of the boys' singles, Liam Broady, from Britain, defeated an Australian, Nick Kyrgios in three sets. These match-ups were to become familiar to Broady as the tournament progressed.

QUOTE of the Day

Australia's Bernard Tomic, who became the youngest quarter-finalist (18) since Boris Becker in 1986 in the men's singles by defeating Xavier Malisse, of Belgium, 6-1 7-5 6-4

"Tennis a sport where anything can happen if you compete well and try. That's what happened in the second round when I was two sets and 2-0 down. Things weren't looking good. I thought it was pretty much over so I decided to compete. Look where I am now."

DAY EIGHT
28.06.2011

Sharapova
vs
Cibulkova

Bartoli
vs
Lisicki

Kvitova
vs
Dironkova

Azarenka
vs
Paszek

Rafael Nadal

TUESDAY 28TH JUNE...

A couple of days before The Championships got underway I had bumped into Rafael Nadal outside the referee's office where he had been sheltering from the elements. He stared up at the leaden skies, rolled his eyes, laid his head on my shoulder in a manner of mock frustration and said he'd had enough of the weather and would walk home and watch Rory McIlroy play some golf.

On the second Tuesday, it was time for McIlroy to return the gesture and come and watch some tennis, though he had picked ladies quarter-finals day for his first venture to the All England Club and decided that a pink tie with his dark suit best fitted the occasion. Nadal was, at the time of McIlroy's arrival, having an MRI scan on the left ankle he had damaged against Juan Martin Del Potro, so was not able to greet someone who had often Tweeted his admiration for the Spaniard.

Before it was time to settle back and watch the actual tennis unfold, we needed to be sure about Rafa's Ankle but it was not until 5.45 pm that he appeared on the practice courts in weather that, had it prevailed in Majorca, he would have promptly shut the door and gone back to his sofa. The No.1 seed appeared at Aorangi Park and if he did not exactly look delighted to be there and engaged in a heated debate with his team about something to which we were not privy, he certainly seemed fit to play the following day.

Over at the practice courts was loitering Giles Smith of *The Times*. "There are 22 courts, arranged in tiers, like vineyards on a mountain, just behind Court No.1 and an angry racket's throw from the car park," he wrote. "On the days when Tracy Austin and Kathy Rinaldi-Stunkel represent a star-spotting breakthrough on the outside courts, Aorangi is the gazer's paradise. Only those at Aorangi know the more intimate experience of watching Andy Murray work on his upper-body strength with a long strip of blue rubber or to marvel at the sheer, heart-chilling oppressively bleak relentlessness that is Victoria Azarenka's practice routine."

Maria Sharapova

This was the last eight of the women's singles and it brought The Championships into a new light. In a sport where the box office was subdued, coincidences and contrivances were bound to be snatched at. With so many top-seeded casualties and the Williams sisters in decline (perhaps), the Tamira Paszek-Azarenka and Petra Kvitova-Tsvetana Pironkova quarter-finals had guaranteed to produce a first-time Grand Slam finalist from one half of the draw.

From Austria, Belarus, Slovakia, Russia, France, Germany, the Czech Republic and Bulgaria eight players were seeking to capitalise on the fluidity in the women's game. Sharapova, a three-time Grand Slam title winner, was the Dame Vera Lynn of this group: a positive veteran of the big moment, which really left her nowhere to hide should she fail to add to the Wimbledon crown she won seven years ago. ➤

Rory McIlroy

Sabine Lisicki

It was time for a reflection on the whys and wherefores of the women's game, so thought the celebrated Paul Hayward of *The Guardian*. "Astonishing statistic, this," he wrote, "if American tennis can claim a share of Sharapova, the semi-finalist who conforms most obviously to male notions of lawn-borne elegance. Among Sharapova's awards from the WTA are Humanitarian of the Year (always a hotly contested title), Most Fashionable Player (On Court), Most Fashionable Player (Off Court) and Most Dramatic Expression. Don't even ask.

"None of the other quarter-finalists could have hoped to match these sparkling decorations, so it was left to them to catch SW19's attention with the quality of their tennis. It was here that Marion Bartoli scored so highly. She argued the case for actually watching the tennis rather than checking out the recognition-ratings of the players."

Bartoli had, indeed accused a few people of 'just thinking about the names' and rightly lauded the entertainment quota of her prospective tussle with Sabine Lisicki. "Woman's tennis just has to have more matches like that, so people will enjoy coming to watch us," Bartoli said "Even though we don't have some big names, some big star names, we are still able to play some good matches. So I think it all depends on the level of intensity we show up on the court with."

Intensity was certainly the watchword for the first match on Centre as first entered Maria Sharapova and, within an hour, she was out of sight once more, her opponent Dominika Cibulkova, of Slovakia, having been crushed beyond measure, 6-1, 6-1. Sharapova did not so much win a match as make a statement - she came out hollering and started hitting a long succession of screamers, scorching the far baseline with a succession of flaming tennis balls. Poor Miss Cbilkova simply did not have an answer to it all.

Sharapova struck 23 winners in that short stint, driving Cibulkova's conveniently flat, hard strokes right back into the corners. Even the serve, the one that had traditionally plagued her and dragged her back from the brink of superstardom, propelled her onward. Sharapova ripped five aces and converted 76% of her first serves, delivering a 110-mph ace in the fifth game of the second set for emphasis. There was but one lonely double fault.

"I still feel I can get a few more miles per hour," Sharapova said. "I think that will come with time." And not only did she win the easy games but the extended ones as well, including one 16-point game in the second set for a break. She was virtually flawless and you had to wonder if, in the absence of the Williams sisters, any of the other semi-finalists had the power, resolve and nerve to play with the former champ. "The tournament's not over," Sharapova insisted. "We still have a few more girls left."

Whoever it was she would play did not appear to matter much. Sharapova had lost her last two meetings with Cibulkova, the most recent just two months ago on clay in Madrid. ➤

Grass was different, though and it is clear Sharapova carries with her the hunger of a woman who required far too long to clamber back to the top.

"I had my success early in my career and I don't regret it," Sharapova said. "I got to learn so much more than players my age. I would have loved to be in the semis and not taken that long, but I'm not complaining. It's the road sometimes you have to take. It's not straight. It has a lot of zig-zags. A lot of times you think it's a dead end."

The second match on Centre would pit Liscki, of Germany, with Marion Bartoli, the French player. The weather turned a decidedly shade of grey, then black. The roof was drawn shut. With thunder and lightning flashing and crashing outside, it all made for a vaguely Wagnerian experience. Dark, heavy and claustrophobic, it could scarcely have been more different from the previous day when the pair had blazed their way to this rendezvous beneath clear blue skies.

From the outset, when she lost the first six points of the match, Bartoli, the No.9 seed, was on the back foot, straining simply to stay in touch, vainly chasing the artful drop shots which followed Lisicki's own-brand thunderbolts. Up in the Royal Box, a decent sand wedge from the action, McIlroy would have appreciated the precision of some of Lisicki's hitting and noted, too, the visible signs of weariness which ultimately proved the hyperactive Bartoli's undoing.

Both players have medically qualified fathers but the Frenchwoman was swift to ➤

supply her own self-diagnosis, having lost 6-4 6-7 6-1. "My mind was trying extremely hard but my body couldn't do anything any more," she sighed afterwards. "I was so exhausted I could barely walk from one side [of the court] to the other. When I slow down it's not a good sign. All of a sudden my body just shut down."

According to her mentor, Nick Bollettieri - the famed American coach whose presence at Wimbledon always shone a light on the place - Lisicki is far from laid-back herself – "It's practice, practice, practice" – but she is increasingly playing smart too. While no one was ever likely to mistake her for an Evonne Goolagong Cawley impersonator, she moved like a genuine athlete and had the necessary stamina to go with it.

Having won the pre-Wimbledon AEGON Classic tournament in Birmingham, she had yet to be beaten on grass this year. As Goran Ivanisevic proved at Wimbledon, ten years earlier, there was no player as fearless as a wild-card pass holder with some momentum. Mix it all together and the echoes of Steffi Graf's glorious past were growing louder.

Yes, Lisicki, 21, stepped off court to be subjected to inevitable (and probably grating) comparisons with Graf, the last German woman to reach a Wimbledon semi-final, in 1999. Graf had been a force of nature: an amalgam of flow and balance and execution. Lisicki is more of a heavy-serving drop-shot addict whose victory over Li has brought her confidence level with her potential. To call her the new Graf, though, was pointlessly to burden her with a responsibility no player should have to bear on the flimsy basis of a common homeland.

Lisicki was joined in the semi-finals by another talented 21-year-old, Kvitova. The Czech Republic No.8 seed hit a staggering 54 winners to the ten managed by Pironkova, winning 6-3 6-7 6-2. Kvitova would now play Azarenka after her match against Tamira Paszek, of Austria, was moved from Court No.1 to Centre Court, under the roof, when rain fell after one game.

Azarenka clearly relished the change in conditions and though there were times when Paszek gave very much as good as she got, the girl from Belarus was simply too strong for her and produced one 'round the net' forehand winner that was one of the most memorable shots of The Championships.

Back in the junior ranks, there was not so much uplifting news for the British camp, for George Morgan, Evan Hoyt, Kyle Edmund, Oliver Hudson and Oliver Golding were all beaten on the same day, just as the dark clouds approached. Golding's defeat was perhaps the most expected for he had learned only a few days earlier that his former coach, the Mexican, Gustavo Perino, had been killed in a car crash. "He was a great guy and I owed him a lot," the teenager from, Surrey said. The lone ranger for Britain in the boys' singles was now Liam Broady, from Stockport.

Victoria Azarenka

DAY NINE
29.06.2011

Tsonga
vs
Federer

A. Murray
vs
Lopez

Djokovic
vs
Tomic

Nadal
vs
Fish

Jo-Wilfried Tsonga
beats Federer

WEDNESDAY 29TH JUNE...

Roger Federer was two sets up on Jo-Wilfried Tsonga on Centre Court, the stuff of matter-of-fact Wimbledon tennis that meant you could pop across the concourse for one of the 60,000 Dutchees sold during The Championships, and by the time you had resumed your seat, it would be 3-0 in the third and that was another Grand Slam semi-final – in Federer's case the 28th of his career – well taken care of.

He had not let a two set lead slip in 178 such major matches in an illustrious life, this was his piece of turf or at least one upon which he had been allowed to park his chaise-longue for five consecutive summers since 2003 until first Rafael Nadal and then, a year ago, Tomas Berdych had tipped him from it.

Tsonga was a hell for leather player but in the first two sets, though the second had required a tie-break to settle it in Federer's favour, nothing seemed untoward and there was certainly no sign of a Swiss malfunction. Then it happened, well perhaps not so much a malfunction as a release of the Tsonga steam engine, a ferocious onslaught of winners and coruscating tennis that caught Federer cold.

Initially, the Frenchman wasted two break points in the third game of the third set but with a huge forehand that clipped the outside of the line, he finally broke serve. There was a distinct shift in the atmosphere on court, for the Federer supporters knew that Tsonga was playing well and there was a suggestion he may be able to maintain focus and keep on converting some fine instinctive shots. He had recently cultivated a one-handed backhand and it flashed across Federer's feet on several occasions. His powerful ground-strokes were instinctively finding the corners.

Most importantly, as he said afterwards, his serve was "unbelievable". After tossing away his first service game, Tsonga did not yield a break point at any point during the match. There was plenty of character, too, to hold at 4-3, 0-30 down. He was again 0-30 down when serving for the set but steadied on his fourth set point to give himself a glimmer of hope. At the end of that set he had requested a comfort break and taken a wrong turning off the court. Once back on it, he did not put a foot wrong.

All the confidence Tsonga was lacking in the early exchanges flowed, he broke in the third game of the fourth set, sending a typically muscular passing shot down the line. He broke again in the first game of the deciding set, proving that fortune favoured the brave with a volleyed lob to take the lead for the first time. It was a grip he simply would not relinquish.

The result meant Federer exited the tournament at the same stage as 2010, when he lost to Tomas Berdych and had thus failed to reach the final for the first time since 2002. But though the Swiss seemed at a loss to explain how Tsonga had found a way back, he said this defeat did not hurt as much as last year's because he had played well.

Tsonga, who ironically had a perfect win record in five-set matches until this season – in which he had lost two – finally delivered on all the promise he has shown in an injury-hit career. "I have improved a lot mentally. I am stronger, I have improved a lot of things in my tennis," he said. "I try to stay focused all the time, just breathe and stay quiet. I did it today and it worked. I am the kind of player who likes these big moments. So I hope I will have some more. I felt so good on the court. I was quick. I was just perfect today. Every time, I was feeling like a dream."

Feliciano Lopez

Of the four men's quarter-finals, this was the result that we had been least prepared for. The other three went according to the seedings, according to the form book and, in one case at least, according to the hopes of the nation. Andy Murray was back in the semi-finals of Wimbledon for a third time, courtesy of a common or garden 6-3 6-4 6-4 victory over Feliciano Lopez, of Spain, which was just about as secure as one might have wanted.

Simon Barnes, of *The Times,* said "I have watched British players on Centre Court on countless occasions but never in an atmosphere such as this. It was as if it was no big deal, a Brit trying to get into a Wimbledon semi-final. Everyone knew he was going to do it. He was a man of confidence and ease was he not? Murray took Lopez apart with detached, surgical precision. He made Lopez look out of his depth, he imposed his authority."

It was, indeed, a superior Murray on the court and Lopez could do next to nothing about it, though some of his play a lot of the time lacked enough conviction for the Scot to have to move to anywhere near to best to quell him. The better matches proved to be played out elsewhere.

On Court No.1, for instance, Novak Djokovic was toiling against the teenager Bernard Tomic, the Australian whose form was delivering fabulous audience viewing figures for Channel 7 which had added Wimbledon to its portfolio for the first time this year. The Australians could probably not quite believe what they were seeing as Tomic, though he lost the first set 6-2, bounded back like Joey the Kangaroo. He also had Patrick Rafter, the Australian Davis Cup captain and Goran Ivanisevic, who like Tomic was a Croatian by birth, in his corner (These two had been the finalists in 2001, for those wondering where they had seen them together before).

Much to Rafter/Ivanisevic delight, Djokovic lost the second set and was close to capitulation in the third before he embarked on a winning streak of five games. He then lost form again, early in the fourth set. "We were playing cat and mouse," the Serb said of he and his opponent, born of Croatian parents. "In the end I was just happy to get through."

Each high reached by 18-year-old Tomic was celebrated vocally by the Australians in the crowd. Dressed in their country's colours of yellow and green, they grew louder as their player grew in confidence, singing "Let's go Bernie, let's go" and yet the teenager, who as a qualifier had played three extra games en route to this quarter-final than Djokovic, hardly seemed fatigued.

That was in stark contrast to the two time semi-finalist, whose body language made him seem a broken man. Throwing his arms to the sky, shaking his head, wiping his brow, falling to the grass and threatening to throw down his racket, at times he looked like he

ROLEX 👑 0.29

SETS GAMES POINTS

TOMIC ● 2

v

OKOVIC 4

S REMAINING
2
IC 3

Novak Djokovic

was wondering where his game had gone. With Tomic taking the second set 6-3 and going 3-1 ahead in the third, how concerned had Djokovic been that he might lose? The Serb shook his head. "No, no, because I believed that I could come back to the match. I thought it's just a period.

"But when you start missing a lot of balls, making a lot of unforced errors, and your opponent is playing well, obviously you lose that comfort zone. I guess that was my case" Djokovic even seemed defensive as he described Tomic's game. "The style of my opponent today is not really something I prefer. He plays very low balls all the time and it's really difficult to predict what he's going to come up with." Djokovic won 6-2 3-6 6-3 7-5.

Following them came Rafael Nadal and Mardy Fish. "Batter him Rafa" was one of the least unexpected cries during the warm up. Perhaps Fish felt exposed by the fact that he seemed to be just about the only person in the arena sensing the slightest tension. With most of the crowd disappearing for a spot of tea, the players had knocked up in the genteel, listless atmosphere of some country house weekend. The storms of the previous day were spent, and high clouds hung benignly above the cool, blue afternoon. As Nadal raced into a 2-0 lead, moreover, the wails and shrieks of excitement from Centre Court suggested no doubt that something rather more competitive was reaching a climax between Federer and Tsonga. ➤

Bernard Tomic

Mardy Fish

The trouble was that Fish's hopes teetered precariously on his first serve. When it was functioning properly, the ball could seldom be retrieved with a mere tennis racket, rather something more in the order of an industrial excavator. Without it, however, the poor man was bereft, his game laid mercilessly bare. Nadal was dismissing second serves with heartless disdain, and Fish managed to win just two of his five service games in the opening set – extended when Nadal had himself inattentively dropped serve at 5-2.

Fish does move gracefully round the court, and his business-like forehand won him a couple of break points in the third game of the second set, but Nadal promptly produced three booming first serves. And that, transparently, would remain the difference between them. Fish did not have the same head for heights. In the very next game he succumbed to a series of downhearted errors, twice finding the net when Nadal was in trouble.

The Spaniard closed out the set in perfunctory fashion, and when he broke serve in the first game of the third, everyone assumed – a bit like Federer and Tsonga after two sets – that the game was up. That unanimity appeared to be shared by his opponent, however, and the American immediately relaxed. The moment the pressure was off, he began to serve and swing lustily. The crowd was thrilled, with the champion finally obliged to turn it on. Nadal, who had been keeping Fish away from the net with those whippy forehands, responded to his new aggression with some lavish crosscourt backhand winners.

Emboldened by a sudden indication of parity, Fish may have begun to wonder about Nadal's injured foot. Suddenly the Spaniard found himself 15-40 down serving at 5-6 in the third. Fish missed his first chance with an overexcited forehand, but smeared the next across the court to land on the chalk. Wearing that sombre scowl of his, Nadal did not take long to retrieve the initiative in the fourth and won 6-3 6-3 5-7 6-4.

There had been an encouraging and bullish run in the men's doubles championships for the unseeded British pair of Colin Fleming and Ross Hutchins. They had defeated the No.7 seeds from Poland, Mariusz Fyrstenberg and Marcin Matkowski in the opening round and were gathering quite a head of steam but it was extinguished in the quarter-finals by an unheralded combination, Christopher Kas, of Germany, and the Austrian, Alexander Peya, 6-4 6-4 6-7 2-6 6-4. Hutchins suffered a bit of a double whammy, losing in the mixed doubles second round with Heather Watson, to Nenad Zimonjic of Serbia and the Slovenian, Katarina Srebotnik, 6-4 6-4.

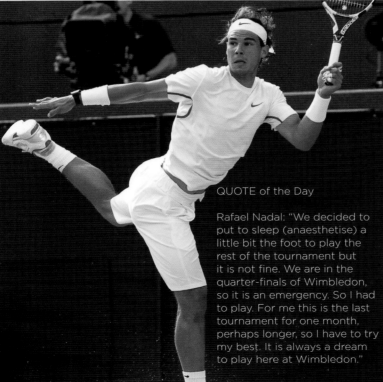

QUOTE of the Day

Rafael Nadal: "We decided to put to sleep (anaesthetise) a little bit the foot to play the rest of the tournament but it is not fine. We are in the quarter-finals of Wimbledon, so it is an emergency. So I had to play. For me this is the last tournament for one month, perhaps longer, so I have to try my best. It is always a dream to play here at Wimbledon."

DAY TEN
30.06.2011

Azarenka
vs
Kvitova

Sharapova
vs
Lisicki

THURSDAY 30TH JUNE...

Having Andy Murray back in a Wimbledon semi-final was the cue for the large percentage of Britain's tennis writers to go in search of any little piece of information, however minute, which might have a bearing on the outcome. Hence, I spent most of the day hanging around the practice courts, seeing if Andy was a) happy b) not very happy c) had he shaved d) who his partner was (Colin Fleming, a right hander which the Spanish press couldn't believe) e) what were the contents of his magic drink and f) I've forgotten what 'f' was now.

The Spaniards did likewise with Rafael Nadal, who practised with a right hander, the British junior and Reed's School attendee, Evan Hoyt, the fair-haired 16-year-old who was now beginning to feel very much part of the Rafa squad which was an interesting dichotomy. Perhaps an unfortunate portent for the outcome on Friday was the sight of Darren Cahill, from Australia, who joined Murray's coaching set up in May had had to pull out of an invitational doubles in the afternoon and was seen limping gingerly along St Mary's Walk.

But we had to rein ourselves back a little because this was women's semi-finals' day, a sea-changing moment we felt, in the ladies' game because we were assured, from one half of the draw to have a new Grand Slam finalist. Would it be Petra Kvitova, of the Czech Republic, or Victoria Azarenka, of Belarus? Indeed, we might have two debutantes, as Sabine Liscki, of Germany, who played Maria Sharapova, was on the cusp of uncharted territory too.

For Azarenka, the recent months had been a trial, going back to the tournament in Doha, where she had lost to Daniela Hantuchova in such a *laissez-faire* fashion that Sam Sumyk, her coach, had demanded that she either pull herself around or their partnership would probably have to come to an end.

With that, and a few days to pull herself around, Azarenka decided to fly home to Minsk and stay with her family. She told them of her dilemma and wondered whether she quite had it in her to be a professional player. "I said I didn't want to do something that I'm not enjoying," she recalled. "My Mum asked ➤

Petra Kvitova

Victoria Azarenka

me: 'What are you going to do?' I said: 'I'm going to study.' She laughed out loud. She knows that I like to study, but I'm not going to be fulfilling that for a long time. I'm just going to get bored, because tennis is what I really love. I just had to take a step back and realise that is true. My mother's a very wise woman. She said: 'Just come back home, enjoy some time, and you decide'.

"My grandmother said: 'if you don't want to do it (tennis) then don't do it. You have to be happy'. She was telling me these stories, about how hard she was working. She had worked in a kindergarten with kids. She'd been doing a lot of work, having two, three jobs at one time. For me, it was like; 'Well, you just have to shut up and stop complaining because you have a pretty damn good life. Just work out there.'"

Azarenka said that as a result of her re-evaluation she had taken on a "completely different" approach to her profession. "I look forward to every challenge and try to be disciplined in what I'm working hard for.

I'm just enjoying myself much more on the court," she said.

The effect on her results were immediate; winning titles in the Sony Ericsson Open in Miami (where she beat five top-25 players, including Kim Clijsters, Vera Zvonareva and Sharapova in the final), reached the last day on the clay in Madrid and made the quarter-finals at the French Open, where she lost to China's Li Na, the eventual champion. En route to the semi finals in SW19, she had only dropped a single set.

She was to start the match against Kvitova a touch too warily. At 3-1 down, she thought she had found a route back into the first set after pulling back to deuce from being 40-0 down to the Czech, but even a two-minute break to quell an alarm that had gone off outside the court could not prevent Kvitova from holding. It was the ferocity of the Kvitova returns that were causing maximum havoc and when she broke for the second time it was the platform for her to unleash three aces in the seventh game to land the set. ➤

Petra Kvitova and Victoria Azarenka

It was imperative that the rot was stopped pretty quickly and Azarenka did just that, winning the first eight points of the second set. There was much shrieking, much fist pumping, much positive energy and the No.4 seed promptly brought the match level, but the up-and-down nature of the match was confirmed in the first game of the final set when Azarenka's head went all fuzzy and she dropped serve after a couple of errant ground-strokes. The nerves were beginning to get to the girl from Belarus again.

Kvitova's coach and her family – plus plenty of new-found friends – a number of whom who made a lot of noise and had extremely long hair – were beginning to get into a right old state as Kvitova, on the back of a delicious drop shot and forehand winner, broke for 4-1, stabilising to lead 5-2 which meant that Azarenka was serving to stay in the tournament. A first match point came and went after a Kvitova forehand error but on the second, Azarenka double faulted. A sad end.

Her own long blonde curls floating down past her shoulders, Kvitova giggled like a schoolgirl as she discussed her win. The 21-year-old's ascent had been remarkable. The No.8 seed was ranked No.62 in the world this time last year and she had never won on grass before she took last year's tournament by storm, reaching a semi-final against Serena Williams. Now she had gone one step further.

"My first memory of Wimbledon as a child was watching Navratilova win here" said Kvitova. Had the legend passed on any helpful hints? "No," she said, shyly. "We spoke about just being here when we met. She told me, 'Good luck, well done.' She was happy when I saw her. I don't know if she can tell me something about the final."

Who would be her opponent there? The answer, which may be of some comfort to the 21-year-old German, Lisicki, as she looked back on her 6-4 6-3 defeat, was that Sharapova dredged up every ounce of her once-familiar competitive ferocity in order to overcome what should have been a crippling self-imposed handicap of 13 double faults (three whole games of double faults).

Back in 2004, Sharapova was already setting new standards for an unflinching readiness to back her own ability to hit the lines with raking drives. "When you're young," she said, "you kind of feel that you've got nothing to lose and you go for it." In a tight spot against Lisicki after the opening games – she was 3-0 down and rocking – she demonstrated that little had changed with the passing years, at least in that important respect.

Not even major surgery in 2008, for a shoulder injury which might have ended her career and which forced her to reconstruct her service action, could persuade her to adopt a more conservative approach to her ground strokes. Virtually every single one is still addressed with maximum venom and the intention of winning the point outright. ➤

Yet when Lisicki won the first three games at a cost of only two points, she must have thought the whole business of reaching the final – even against a former champion – was a ridiculously easy affair. Sharapova said, "The first three games she played very well and I did quite the opposite. And then I told myself to take it one point at a time and really focus." In the next game Lisicki had three opportunities for a second break, but failed to take advantage as her opponent began to find her range and exert pressure in the rallies.

Sharapova had conceded her first service game with a double fault, and soon Lisicki's own serve – one of the most dangerous on the WTA tour – was starting to let her down. The high kick of her second delivery was a useful weapon, but the 6ft 2in Russian on the other side of the net was able to get on top of it and send it back with interest. With the constant vocal encouragement of her fiance, Sasha Vujacic, the New Jersey Nets shooting guard, Sharapova was setting up rallies in which her scorching drives pulled the world No.62 from one side of the baseline to the other, provoking the first trickle of what became a steady stream of errors.

Kvitova believed her best weapon against the Russian in the final would be her left-handed serve. "I have a good serve," she said, explaining it did not come naturally, but instead took three years of hard coaching to perfect. "And I'm not afraid of volleying because we practised with my father when I was young."

In the boy's singles, on strode Liam Broady, the 17-year-old from Stockport, into the semi-finals. And yet, his father, Simon, and the LTA chief executive Roger Draper did not exactly see eye-to-eye. There was confirmation, too, that Nigel Sears, the head women's coach, was departing HQ.

"There will always be those who disagree with strategies and policies and you want as many people as possible heading in the right direction," Draper said. "While I don't like the situation at the moment with Simon Broady because it's not positive for the sport, there are always parents like that who are around. There will always be people who disagree with your coaching strategy, who say mini tennis is a load of rubbish and we should use full courts for 6-year-olds. But our juniors coming out of mini tennis are some of the best in Europe and the best in the world.

"It's balancing all of those feelings. Of course, we have made mistakes, are our 3,000 coaches absolutely behind what we are doing, probably not. We are on a big engagement programme with those coaches but you're not going to get every parent and coach, partner or politician agreeing. But you have to try and work through that and be as positive with those people as possible." ℰ

Maria Sharapova

DAY ELEVEN
01.01.2011

A. Murray
vs
Nadal

Djokovic
vs
Tsonga

Broady
vs
Kubler

FRIDAY 1ST JULY...

The Thunderer duly thundered. "There are 27 million males in Britain, of whom 5.6 million are below the age of 16 and 14.8 million are above the age of 35. Britain, therefore, has just shy of seven million men who are in the right age bracket for a life as a top-class professional sportsman. The great diversity of human interests — the tendency of some men to read books or play in orchestras — rules out a good proportion of that seven million.

"Of the millions left who love sport in all its guises, too many, alas, have everything they need with the exception of talent. The set of young men who might conceivably be candidates for a career in sport is already vanishing. For all these reasons, it is not a failure but a victory against the odds for a young Scotsman to be the fourth-best tennis player in the world and play in three consecutive semi-finals at Wimbledon. And if and when it all goes wrong, at least we can look forward to the Olympic small-bore shooting next year. The Australians are hopeless."

The morning after another setback in the semi-finals of Wimbledon was always one of the harshest of days but this one particularly so. Andy Murray had been in charge of a match against Rafael Nadal and that was the case at this level of a major championship only once before, the 2008 US Open when a change of weather and a court shift could not undermine Murray's progress to a four set victory and his first and ultimately fruitless Grand Slam final appearance.

Think about what was happening on Centre Court at around 5.45 pm. Murray led Nadal by a set, 2-1 and was 15-30 on the Spaniard's serve. There were certain signs that the champion was not happy, his dark glances to his corner for one, the ever-so slightly longer preparation time he was taking, the fact that when he planted his right foot just behind the service line, he was having difficulty retaining his balance. He had come over all wobbly.

At that moment, an American colleague reached across two folk in the press benches to announce that he had never seen Murray playing this well. I swallowed hard. As so much in this world, timing was everything. On the subsequent point, in which Nadal just managed to stay to hoist an inadequate defensive shot, Murray could have played ten different types of forehand and he would have won the point. Unfortunately, he decided upon an 11th. That was it, right there and then. 15-40 was instead, 30-all, Nadal had been reprieved and you did not reprieve Nadal without paying a heavy price.

And so it was that he, who had not lost here in four years and 20 matches, won 5-7 6-2 6-2 6-4 and, for Murray, the depths were hard to deal with. After one of the quickest cooldowns of his career, probably, Murray faced the media and said of his second-set gaffe: "It was a big point. I was playing very high-risk tennis for most of the match. I started making a few mistakes, but a match that lasted nearly ➤

three hours [to turn] on one point... I slightly overhit that one. A year ago they were saying I was playing too defensively, today I was going for all my shots."

True, there had often been a pronounced passivity from Murray when urgency was required and it was striking that balance, the gung-ho versus the go-lightly that was his constant inner battle. Nadal, ever the gracious winner said later: "I said, 'sorry for that' (the forehand error) to him. I had to play my best tennis to have any chance. He's a great champion. He was playing fantastic at the beginning, he made an important mistake at 15-30 and 2-1 up at the start of the second. That was a turning point."

Nadal mentioned luck but Murray was not really listening. In truth, the champ was being a bit kind. That mistake did more than cost Murray a break, it broke his concentration, flooded his mind with doubt and, to an extent, the rhythm that drives his superb shot-making. As Murray gradually folded, 38 unforced errors dribbling from his racket, Nadal (who astoundingly made none at all in the second set and only seven in all) raised his game to a level beyond anything he had played in this 125th Wimbledon, and some way out of reach of the world No.4.

Kevin Mitchell, of the *Guardian*, set the scene and described the opening exchanges. "Before a ball was struck, they slipped into type; as the little-bull Spaniard sprinted to the back of the court, legs pumping in anticipation of a fight, the diffident Scot, sporting perhaps the worst facial growth outside a circus, was still doing up his shoelaces at the net, distracted in a schoolboy's way. Not so when he got down to business: in the 55 minutes of the first set, Murray battered Nadal's backhand until his shoulder ached. He won the first game inside a minute, banging two of his 15 aces. The gathering stirred. "I love you Andy," cried a plaintive male (English, possibly Surrey) voice from the stands, sounding suspiciously like the one that had plucked at Djokovic's heart strings a couple of hours earlier – but the love game was Nadal's, behind a precise, clean serve".

Indeed, Murray's had clicked lethally, and a couple of aces got him to 4-3 after half an hour. Serving to stay in the set, Nadal was struggling against the British player's patient, pressure tennis, and remained largely stuck on the baseline. Murray earned three set points by working the Spaniard's backhand relentlessly. When Nadal's sliced backhand struck the net, a piercing roar filled the court and Murray was 7-5 up and flying.

Then came 'the' error. Then, Murray could not make a relatively straightforward overhead that might have prevented Nadal breaking for a 3-2 lead, the crowd gulped and Nadal proceeded to win the next five games in succession – all of this error free. Would an unlikely running forehand winner from Murray succeed in galvanising him, even though he trailed 3-2 in the third set? No, because Nadal held with ease, grabbed a new racket from his

bag, broke serve once more, gobbled a banana almost whole and wrested complete control with an early break at the start of the fourth set. Cue the inevitable wholesale British woe.

It would not be hyperbole to have described the first semi-final of the day, between Novak Djokovic and Jo-Wilfried Tsonga as entertainment of the highest level. How often do you see both players prostrate on either side of the net, having thrown themselves horizontally in an attempt to keep a point alive? How often does a semi-final victor fall to his knees and plant a smacker on the court? And yet, after the first set had been pocketed by him, did anyone seriously consider that Djokovic would have been denied his second Grand Slam final of the year?

This was memorable fare because almost every point stretched both protagonists to the limit. Tsonga, who lost 7-6 6-2 6-7 6-3 said he could have beaten anyone that day bar the 'unbelievable' Serbian. He had won all of those matches, he had gathered a hard-edge to his tennis and his decision to bypass the Queen's Club tournament in the week immediately after the completion of his clay court exertions was looking more and more like a master-stroke.

Djokovic had to be at his most alert, agile and relentless. And yet it all began so unpromisingly for the 24-year-old, with Tsonga emerging into the sunlight as if he had been crowned, that very morning, the best grass-court player of all time. In the sixth game of the opening set there was an exchange that ranked as the most fun-filled and delightful of The Championships as both slipped, skidded and stretched with deadly accuracy, Tsonga emerging the victor to rapturous applause. He responded by turning to the Royal Box and holding out his arms in the style of Wayne Rooney after his scissor-kick goal at Old Trafford last season.

"I don't remember everything," Tsonga said when asked to pick his best shot of the match. In truth, there were too many to relate and he should, as he intimated he might, watch the DVD to remind himself of its finer moments. Tsonga decided to split with Éric Winogradsky, his coach, in April and to take a more intuitive approach to his training, putting in the hours when he felt like it, resting when it suited him, leaving decisions to the morning they are needed rather than following a timetable.

Yet, he was probably undone in part by his decision-making, approaching the net on occasions when it was unsafe to do so and failing to punish his opponent's second serve. Few watching wanted him to become more conservative, however; it was simply wonderful entertainment just as it was — even if the No.12 seed seemed doomed to heroic failure.

Djokovic's relentless ability to cover the court and hold his nerve was at the crux of his win. The Serb could have wrapped the tie up sooner when the incredibly tense third-set tie-break swerved from offering a match point to set point and back again, but Tsonga held firm much to the crowd's delight. They had fallen for Tsonga the showman.

The scoreboard reads:

Jo-Wilfried TSONGA ● 0 2 40
62
4
v
76
Novak DJOKOVIC 2 4 30

CHALLENGES REMAINING
J. TSONGA   3
N. DJOKOVIC   3

"I don't have any problem with the crowds," Tsonga said, "If you give to them, they give to you." Even when 5-2 down in the fourth set and serving to stay in the match, the man who knocked out Federer in the previous round kept on giving. His lob under pressure kept the tie alive, briefly, and was an appropriate sign-off for a new Centre Court hero, albeit a gallant loser. At the net the two men embraced in acknowledgement of their respective efforts.

Djokovic's camp went into an immediate huddle and jumped in unison with delight as their man at last let his emotions out for they knew that their new, improved, serious Serb had turned into an extremely hard a man to beat.

Over on Court No.2, the fair-haired Liam Broady – having beaten Jason Kubler of Australia 6-4, 6-3 – had become the first player to reach the final of the boy's singles since Miles Kasiri in 2004, so there was a ray of sunshine on a cloudy day for the British game. Everyone in British tennis took their cue from Murray, as did Broady's coach, Mark Hilton "This is just the start of the journey for Liam," the former British international said. "He is a rough diamond. It's important that he does the right things with his physique, you only have to see how Andy had developed physically to realise the levels of work Liam needs to do. The next three years are critical."

Above: Winner of The Rolex Wimbledon Picture of the Year Competition 2011

Photographer: Glyn Kirk

QUOTE of the Day

Andy Murray on the blow of another semi-final defeat to Rafael Nadal

"I'll work harder than I did before and try to improve and get stronger. Be more professional. Try to learn from what happened today. Tennis right at the top of the game is exceptional. I need to work 2 or 3% harder and push myself to be the best athlete that I can be, in practice, in my diet, the gym, the training I do."

DAY TWELVE
02.07.2011

Sharapova
vs
Kvitova

Broady
vs
Saville

Bryan and Bryan
vs
Lindstedt and Tecau

Peschke and
Srebotnik
vs
Stosur and Lisicki

Petra Kvitova

SATURDAY 2ND JULY...

Petra Kvitova and Maria Sharapova stood in the Centre Court waiting room before the ladies' singles final. Actually it's not really a waiting room, it's more of a lobby, but they waited and waited and waited a bit longer. Something was obviously not quite right with the timings on court because one had never seen such a delay before such an occasion until they were let out into the light.

Perhaps it had something to do with the massive infestation of greenfly that had descended on SW19 with a furore that took the breath away – actually when these pesky aphids got into your mouth, they did take the breath away. Rafael Nadal was forced off court during a practice session as a cloud of the insects swarmed around him. Liam Broady and Luke Saville, of Australia, his opponent in the boys' final were seen swatting the bugs away with their rackets between points.

(There were reports of greenfly harassing shoppers in Leicester city centre with pedestrians forced to fight their way through a swarm. Scientist, Richard Harrington, said he believed this year's infestation was the biggest for five years and numbers would stay high until the end of the cereal harvest. He blamed the rise on the cold winter, which meant aphid numbers were abnormally low in spring and populations of the insects that feed on them, ladybirds, lacewings and hover flies, were weakened, so when the greenfly made a comeback after the hot, late spring there were fewer natural predators around).

This was interesting up to a point but it certainly made for an unusual preparation for one of the game's showpieces as those sitting on the show courts were forced to use the copies of their newspapers for more than digesting the form of the competitors.

For those who were keen to know, Kvitova had been barely four months old when Martina Navratilova swept aside Zina Garrison, of the United States, to win her ninth Wimbledon singles in 1990 and her 18th in total. Yet their paths would cross, their lives connect. Like Navratilova, Kvitova was Czech and when she started tennis people spoke to her about Navratilova. "Like her, you're a left-hander." Still it was a stretch to imagine Kvitova could come to Wimbledon at age 21, just as Navratilova had done, and win her first Grand Slam title.

And Navratilova was present to witness what we might have termed "Petra's first". Because you could bet your pension on it: there would be others. There was so much to admire about the way she played and dealt with an occasion that would have overwhelmed plenty in her position.

It was her first experience of Centre Court in these circumstances and yet there was no retreat into timidity, and no suggestion of inferiority from a young woman whom

Maria Sharapova

the bookmakers and many others did not expect to win. "Sometimes," Maria Sharapova was to say after the 6-3 6-3 defeat that set off a wave of Czech jubilation, "you play your best because you have that feeling of nothing to lose." Sharapova could not, on this occasion, have been more wrong. Kvitova was no outsider casting caution to the wind, or playing with the daredevilry of the loser-to-be. Rather, she played like she saw herself as favourite and at most of the big moments, she produced winners that rocked the Russian and challenged every pre-conceived notion that Sharapova was the likely winner.

This was not how you expected a 21-year-old debutante to play a final of this magnitude and it was that ability to play her most aggressive shots at critical points in the match that defined her performance. The story of the match was foretold in the first two games; Kvitova hit a tentative forehand into the net to lose her service in the opening game but then, straight off, she returned Sharapova's service with such power and penetration that you wondered if the favourite would ever hold her serve.

Going into the final she had unleashed 214 clean winners to Sharapova's 140 and once she settled into her game after an understandably nervy start, the degree of superiority was relative to the pair's progression to the climax. The proportion of left-handers to right is far smaller on the women's tour than the men's; indeed there had only been three southpaw Wimbledon ladies finalists in the Open era (Navratilova, Ann Jones and Monica Seles).

"She used that to her advantage a lot," admitted Sharapova. "She was hitting really powerful winners from all over the court. She made a defensive shot into an offensive one. She was just more aggressive than I was, hit deeper and harder, and got the advantage."

Sharapova won the title seven years ago by virtue of a classic service action, but her delivery has descended into something of a lottery following that shoulder surgery in 2008. Double faults allowed Kvitova the break to take command of the first set at 4-2.

Kvitova was repeatedly hitting forehands to the body of Sharapova, who in turn struggled to find any consistency on her ground strokes. Balls were flying beyond the baseline by a yard or more and the Czech was looking to up the pace. A poor game allowed Sharapova back into contention at 3-3 in the second set but Kvitova immediately shrugged off her disappointment and that ➤

was effectively the last seen of the three-time former champion.

However, the best of all was saved for the grand finale, as Barry Flatman of the *Sunday Times* wrote. "If Kvitova was nervous as she stepped up to serve for the title, she refused to let even a trace of her anxiety show. First she smote a strong backhand winner into the far angle of the court, next she extended a beaten Sharapova from one extreme of the baseline to the other and finally she moved to match point with an unplayable delivery her opponent could only strike into the net.

"After hitherto failing to unleash any of her trademark aces throughout the final, the ball that propelled Kvitova on to a grandiose roll of honour shot down the middle of the playing arena and past Sharapova's outstretched racket at an unstoppable 105mph. The new champion's timing was precise, and the applause welcomed a new and opportune star."

Once he had swatted away the greenfly, Liam Broady, found that the rugged determination of his Australian opponent, Luke Saville, was harder to contend with in the boy's singles final, a 2-6 6-4 6-2 defeat rather mirroring Andy Murray's demise against Nadal the day earlier, an early period of dominance, a fluctuation and the opposition disappearing over the horizon.

Whether Broady could progress from his ranking of No.756 into the top 100 would depend on the strength of his mind, the development of his physique, the support of those around him and the odd stroke of luck. "It's so hard to judge," said David Felgate, who once coached Tim Henman from the depths of the rankings to challenge for the Grand Slams. "You look at his physique, his temperament and his technique. Has he got room to develop? How did he handle himself on court? It's a big leap from the 700s even up into the 400s and 300s."

Though he had handled the sudden attention with the coolness of a veteran, Broady must have been mesmerised by a crowd 20 times bigger than any before in his experience. The ATP Futures circuit to whence he was heading attracted few spectators and the players were hardly in the lap of luxury. There would be an umpire but no ball collectors and certainly no Hawk-Eye. It was tennis stripped down to the basics but the costs of travelling and accommodation were still prohibitive to those outside the system. The Broadys could not afford to go to the Australian Open in January.

Broady's game had plenty to commend it. His sliding left-hander's serve to the advantage court caused the gangling Australian real problems through the opening set and a half, while Broady was also more

Liam Broady (left) and Luke Saville

consistent off the ground on both wings. His forehand was a nicely grooved stroke, hit, for the most part, to a consistent length and his two-handed backhand is flat and powerful. Weapons enough to give hope for the future.

Bob and Mike Bryan added to the reasons for being recognised in tennis' hall of fame when they won their eleventh Grand Slam men's doubles title with a 6-3 6-4 7-6 win over Sweden's Robert Lindstedt and Horia Tecau, from Romania. The Californian lefty-righty twins, who were told by their parents not to compete for real when they faced each other in tournaments, long ago became an eye-catching duo.

After quitting singles entirely they had gone on to win at least one Grand Slam title every year since 2003, to accumulate the complete set of four majors, and to surpass Mark Woodforde's and Todd Woodbridge's – the Woodies – record of 61 titles. Now they had equalled the Australians' record of the most number of Grand Slam men's doubles titles in the Open era, doing so with an economical victory which was a relief after their marathon third round and semi-final survivals in five sets.

"To equal the Woodies, a team that we idolised, the greatest team in our mind, is unbelievable. I mean, to get their title record and get the Grand Slam record, I mean, I'm

Bob and Mike Bryan

trying to figure out what's left," said Mike. "Those guys have been really gracious. They're the first to come up to us and congratulate us. Mark came to L.A. when we broke the 61 record." It was important that the Bryans got an early break in both the first two sets, both because they were a good front running team, and also because they were unsure how much energy they had left.

They say that perseverance pays off and that was certainly true of the ladies' doubles champions, Katarina Srebotnik, of Slovenia, and her partner, Kveta Peschke, of the Czech Republic. Having lost in four Grand Slam finals before, including the 2007 final when she

played with Japan's Ai Sugiyama, Srebotnik was especially thrilled to have earned her spurs and in some style. She and Peschke defeated Samantha Stosur, of Australia, and Sabine Lisicki, the ladies' singles semi-finalist from Germany, 6-3 6-1. "This is the cherry on the cake," said Peschke. "We have played magnificently through the whole year and great in the final today. We're so happy to have a trophy, this trophy, in our hands."

Not only were they a fine doubles team, they also did pretty well in completing each others sentences. Peschke: "It's a special moment. Srebotnik: "It's special no matter how you look at it. It has some…" Peschke "Magic."

Czech Republic's Kveta Peschke and Slovenia's Katarina Srebotnik celebrate their victory

FINAL DAY
03.07.2011

Nadal
vs
Djokovic

Melzer and Benesova
vs
Bhupathi and Vesnina

Barty
vs
Khromacheva

Cash and Woodforde
vs
Bates and Jarryd

Golding and Vesely
vs
Morgan and Pavic

Vergeer and Walraven
vs
Griffioen and van Koot

Scheffers and Vink
vs
Houdet and Jeremiasz

Navratilova and Novotna
vs
Davenport and Hingis

Schuurs and Tang
vs
Bouchard and Min

Bjorkman and Woodbridge
vs
Eltingh and Haarhuis

Buis and Sevenans
vs
Shuker and Whiley

Ammerlaan and Olsson
vs
Egberink and Kunieda

SUNDAY 3RD JULY...

Martina Navratilova took a blade of it and, hoping not too many people noticed, stuffed it quickly into her racket bag; Bjorn Borg, returning to Centre Court after a near 20 year absence for the Champions' Parade in 2000, briefly knelt and kissed the ground upon which he had run himself into the folklore of the sport. He was so so quick that the TV cameras missed the moment. Most people contented themselves with falling on it, rolling in it, going down on their knees upon it or, in the olden days, simply leaping the net that divided one player from the other.

On the moment of his coronation as the 65th holder of the gentleman's singles title at the All England Club, Novak Djokovic did what none of the others had ever done (so far as we know). He ate the grass! Not all of it mind, but enough for it to taste, one would imagine, somewhere between nectar and caviar.

Djokovic was the first Serbian champion, ten years after the first Croatian, Goran Ivanisevic, but rather than having been invited back by The Championships as a mark of its respect for him coming so close on so many occasions, Djokovic was the player of the year to date, a man who, with his victory over

Rafael Nadal 6-4 6-1 1-6 6-3 in the final, had tasted defeat (rather than grass) just once in 51 of his previous competitive matches and that was in the French Open semi-finals.

If ever a man deserved to be the Wimbledon champion for all that he had put into the task of winning it, then Djokovic, the 24-year-old from Belgrade was very much that man. He could not be begrudged, even if it was Nadal, who had worked so hard to become a man of the people, who had to bow to him again.

Remarkably, this was the fifth final in succession in which Djokovic had beaten Nadal and to rub salt into the Spanish wounds, he would also become No.1 for the first time the day after the final, though his ascension had been secured once he won the quarter-finals. Such finer points mattered not to him.

In the course of planning *The Times* Wimbledon supplement, I had chatted with Djokovic the day before the tournament, in one of the cosy one-on-one interview rooms across the way from Centre Court. "I was considered among the best when I won the Australian Open in 2008," he recalled. "They said 'Wow, this guy is really serious, and then I did my imitations and they said 'He likes having fun and he's outgoing'. And then I had my mini crisis, with some ups and downs in results – for example in 2010 I wasn't able to get to a single final of a Masters 1000 event – and they began to write me off," he said.

"It was very much a struggle for me. Not easy. Everything changes with the way you are performing and that's natural. I've accepted that as a part of my life. I go through problems with my private life every day just like everybody else. I thought I could separate the two (private from professional) but it's impossible. It's all a lesson and a test from God."

My admiration for him went up another notch that day and a few further as the tournament progressed. By the time he was cradling the golden cup and making his way with it to all corners of Centre Court on July 3, it was hard to feel anything but the deepest of regard.

The atmosphere before the start was as tense and febrile as could be imagined. Here were the two young masters of the new order about to meet on the most famous of battlegrounds. When Nadal reached 15-30 on Djokovic's serve in the very first game, the court buzzed as it usually does before such a point. The Serbian got himself out of that awkward position and was on his way.

Throughout the first set he pressed Nadal with increasing vigour, his movement sharper and his hitting harder. There was a terse authority about his play that precluded moments of fantasy but made life awfully difficult for the man with 10 Grand Slam titles to his name. With Nadal serving at 4-5, Djokovic saw his opportunity and concluded two long rallies with crushing forehands whose effects seemed to carry over into the next game, when the Spaniard's errors forfeited the set.

Djokovic took Nadal's serve again at the start of the second set and resisted the attempted break-back with his best tennis of the match, interrupted only by his own applause for a staggering forehand winner from his opponent, before harrying his way to a two-set lead. There were some of us who could not recall when we had seen a better set, certainly one with so much at stake against such an opponent.

After that it was little surprise that he relaxed involuntarily, enabling Nadal to scramble his way back into the contest. But the great Mallorcan has not been at his best in this tournament – those painkilling injections in his foot alone have knocked a couple of percentage points off his effectiveness and movement – and Djokovic was able to re-establish the sort of command he had enjoyed in the earlier stages.

How important, though, had been a single overhead on the sixth point of the fourth set? Miss it and Nadal would have had a break and perhaps a compelling surge of adrenalin but Djokovic did not miss, Nadal's forehand skimmed long and he held. Indeed, he broke in the second game but after an 18-bounce preparation on break point in the third game, he sent down a poor serve, Nadal's return hit the top of the net and it had been retrieved. ➤

But the old champ was still not quite there, serving a double fault at the start of the eighth game. Djokovic broke, delivered a backhand cross-court volley behind a serve to set up match point (bravery indeed) and was a Nadal backhand error away from being fulfilled as never before.

He started this season with one Grand Slam victory to his name, in Australia three years ago, and his mother, Dijana, had said that it was last year's Davis Cup victory which helped unlock his full potential. "If my mother says that, then it's like that, you know?" he said on Sunday night, laughing aloud. "There's nothing else I can say. Mother knows me better than I know myself. No, it really is. After the Davis Cup I was full of life, full of energy, eager to come back to the tennis court, eager to play some more and win some other tournaments. In a sentence, I lost my fear."

The thoughts of Marian Vajda, his coach, were equally fascinating "This year was the year he dominated so much but I have to go back a little bit back into the past when Novak was not able to challenge the top guys that much," the Slovakian said. "He was struggling with his serve at the start of 2010, then if you don't find your game through the serve, you basically cannot play. He was managing to keep up on third place but the mental strength was not there because his game had almost collapsed, he couldn't find the rhythm and it was tough to play without the serve. It takes a long time, even if he is such a talent.

"The breakthrough was definitely Davis Cup but we had the procedure as usual. I have been with him five years but we changed some things, he improved his serve, his forehand. He realised he had to get his fitness better, he can breathe better, he can stay there longer, he can work harder. After the Australian Open victory, we obviously set our sights on winning the French Open and Wimbledon and accordingly, we adjusted our schedule. But, in that period, he found himself in every way." Nadal simply accepted defeat in his typically gracious way and said he would be back to fight another day.

In the mixed doubles championship, there was a notable victory for Jurgen Melzer, of Austria, and Iveta Benesova, of the Czech Republic who defeated India's Mahesh Bhupathi and Elena Vesnina, of Russia, the No.4 seeds. It took them just 51 minutes to win 6-3 6-2 completing an entire tournament without dropping a set. The victory represented a first at this level for Benesova, though Melzer had landed the men's doubles title a year earlier with Philipp Petzschner, of Germany. For the 37-year-old Bhupathi, however, the wait for his eighth Grand Slam mixed doubles crown would go on.

There was a remarkable story in the final of the girl's singles when Ashleigh Barty defeated Irina Khromacheva, of Russia, 7-5 7-6 to become the first indigenous Australian since Evonne Goolagong to make a dramatic impact on the tennis stage – and what better place for young Ashleigh to make her mark than the scene of five finals and two titles by the player who became Mrs Roger Cawley.

Barty was only a year older than Laura Robson, when the then 14-year-old Australian-born English player won the title in 2008 and she went home to be celebrated for one of the nations famed 'Deadly Awards' which celebrates indigenous achievement. The finalists for sportswoman of the year, announced on a blast from a didgeridoo outside the Sydney Opera House, included young Ashleigh.

It was a considerable success, too, for Jason Stoltenberg, the 1996 Wimbledon singles semi-finalist (he lost to the eventual champion, Richard Krajicek) who had been coaching Ashleigh alongside Nicole Pratt. "They have been able to share their experiences, especially Jason with what he had done at Wimbledon," the new champion said. "He also coached Lleyton Hewitt to world No.1 so to be able to talk to these guys about what it takes is really special."

There was a stirring final to the girls' doubles before the No.2 seeds, Grace Min, of the USA, and Canada's Eugenie Bouchard defeated Demi Schuurs, of the Netherlands, and Hao Chen Tang, of China, 5-7 6-2 7-5 in an hour and 48 minutes.

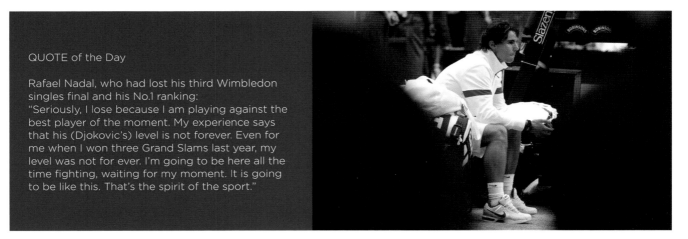

QUOTE of the Day

Rafael Nadal, who had lost his third Wimbledon singles final and his No.1 ranking:
"Seriously, I lose because I am playing against the best player of the moment. My experience says that his (Djokovic's) level is not forever. Even for me when I won three Grand Slams last year, my level was not for ever. I'm going to be here all the time fighting, waiting for my moment. It is going to be like this. That's the spirit of the sport."

Ashleigh Barty

Martina Navratilova and Jana Novotna

George Morgan

Eugenie Bouchard
and Grace Min

Britain rejoiced in that the final of the boys' doubles was bound to provide a home success as George Morgan, from Bolton, had teamed with Croatian, Mate Pavic, to play Oliver Golding and Jiri Vesely, of the Czech Republic. In the tussle of two left-right handed combinations, Morgan and Pavic, who were seeded No.2 toppled the top seeds in another enthralling contest 3-6 6-4 7-5.

"We kept saying to each other 'stay positive, we know we can win,'" Morgan, who won the Orange Bowl under-18 title in Florida late last year, said. "It was right up among the best feelings of my career, winning a tight match on a big court (No.1) against a couple of very good players."

A special place remained, still at The Championships for the veterans of the game, those who had enthralled in the past and kept on enthralling. Jacco Eltingh and Paul Haarhuis, of the Netherlands, could still pass for players on the tour now, as could the pair they defeated in the gentlemen's invitational doubles, Todd Woodbridge, of Australia (who was working for Channel 7 as well as being the head of mens' development in his home nation) and Jonas Bjorkman, of Sweden, who was also carving out a career in television. The Dutchmen won 3-6 6-3, (13-11 in the champions' tie-break).

There were 27 Grand Slam singles titles between the four competitors in the ladies invitational doubles final, which was won 6-4 6-4 by Lindsay Davenport, of the USA, and Martina Hingis, of Switzerland, against the pair of Czech Republic-born champions, Martina Navratilova and Jana Novotna.

The senior gentlemen's invitational doubles was won by Pat Cash, the 1987 men's singles champion, and his Australian compatriot, Mark Woodforde, 6-3 5-7 (10-5 in the champions' tie-break) over Britain's Jeremy Bates and Anders Jarryd, of Sweden.

As an understated element of the game, the wheelchair players continued to take the breath away with their extraordinary skill and strength. Wimbledon had embraced the significance of their play since 2005 when the first gentlemen's doubles event was played and the champions this year were, in the event's two sections, Ronald Vink and Maikel Scheffers, of The Netherlands, the top seeds, who defeated Stephane Houdet and Michael Jeremiasz, of France, 7-5 6-2; and the unseeded Robin Ammerlaan, of Holland and his Swedish partner, Stefan Olsson, 6-3 6-3 winners over Tom Egberink, also from Holland and Shingo Kunieda, of Japan.

Few players had adorned the wheelchair game more than Holland's Esther Vergeer and she became a Wimbledon champion for the third time, once more in partnership with Sharon Walvaren who defeated their compatriots, Jiske Griffioen and Aniek Van Koot 6-4 3-6 7-5. In the second section, Marjolein Buis, another Dutch player, teamed with Annick Sevenans, from Belgium, and toppled the British pair, Lucy Shuker and Jordanne Whiley, 6-3 7-6.

Novak Djokovic
The Gentlemen's Singles

Petra Kvitova
The Ladies' Singles

Bob Bryan & Mike Bryan
The Gentlemen's Doubles

Kveta Peschke & Katarina Srebotnik
The Ladies' Doubles

Jurgen Melzer & Iveta Benesova
The Mixed Doubles

Jacco Eltingh & Paul Haarhuis
The Gentlemen's Invitation Doubles

Eugenie Bouchard & Grace Min
The Girls' Doubles

Mate Pavic & George Morgan
The Boys' Doubles

Pat Cash & Mark Woodforde
The Gentlemen's Senior Invitation Doubles

Martina Hingis & Lindsay Davenport
The Ladies' Invitation Doubles

Ashleigh Barty
The Girls' Singles

Luke Saville
The Boys' Singles

Sharon Walraven & Ester Vergeer
The Wheelchair Ladies' Invitation Doubles

Maikel Scheffers & Ronald Vink
The Wheelchair Gentlemen's Invitation Doubles

CHAMPIONSHIP
RECORDS 2011

EVENT I – THE GENTLEMEN'S SINGLES CHAMPIONSHIP 2011
HOLDER: RAFAEL NADAL

The Winner became the holder, for the year only, of the CHALLENGE CUP presented by The All England Lawn Tennis and Croquet Club in 1887. The Winner received a silver replica of the Challenge Cup. A Silver Salver was presented to the Runner-up and a Bronze Medal to each defeated Semi-finalist. The matches were the best of five sets.

Heavy type denotes seeded players. The figure in brackets against names denotes the order in which they were seeded.
The figures in italics denotes ATP Ranking – (WC)=Wild card. (Q)=Qualifier. (LL)=Lucky loser.

EVENT II – THE GENTLEMEN'S DOUBLES CHAMPIONSHIP 2011
HOLDERS: JURGEN MELZER & PHILIPP PETZSCHNER

The Winners became the holders, for the year only, of THE CHALLENGE CUPS presented by the OXFORD UNIVERSITY LAWN TENNIS CLUB in 1884 and the late SIR HERBERT WILBERFORCE in 1937. The Winners received a silver replica of the Challenge Cup. A Silver Salver was presented to each of the Runners-up, and a Bronze Medal to each defeated Semi-finalist. The matches were the best of five sets.

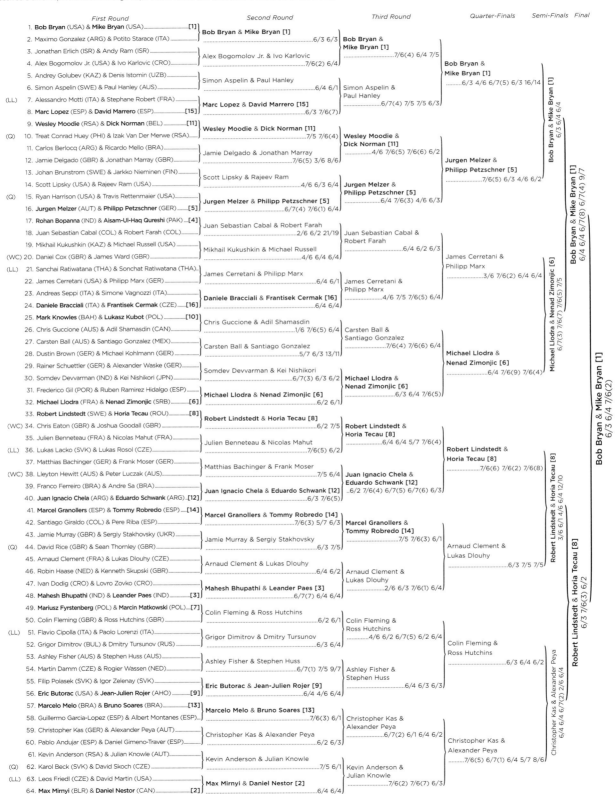

	First Round	Second Round	Third Round	Quarter-Finals	Semi-Finals	Final

1. **Bob Bryan** (USA) & **Mike Bryan** (USA)......[1]
2. Maximo Gonzalez (ARG) & Potito Starace (ITA)
3. Jonathan Erlich (ISR) & Andy Ram (ISR)
4. Alex Bogomolov Jr. (USA) & Ivo Karlovic (CRO)
5. Andrey Golubev (KAZ) & Denis Istomin (UZB)
6. Simon Aspelin (SWE) & Paul Hanley (AUS)
(LL) 7. Alessandro Motti (ITA) & Stephane Robert (FRA)
8. **Marc Lopez** (ESP) & **David Marrero** (ESP) [15]
9. Wesley Moodie (RSA) & Dick Norman (BEL) [11]
(Q) 10. Treat Conrad Huey (PHI) & Izak Van Der Merwe (RSA)
11. Carlos Berlocq (ARG) & Ricardo Mello (BRA)
12. Jamie Delgado (GBR) & Jonathan Marray (GBR)
13. Johan Brunstrom (SWE) & Jarkko Nieminen (FIN)
14. Scott Lipsky (USA) & Rajeev Ram (USA)
(Q) 15. Ryan Harrison (USA) & Travis Rettenmaier (USA)
16. **Jurgen Melzer** (AUT) & **Philipp Petzschner** (GER) [5]
17. **Rohan Bopanna** (IND) & **Aisam-Ul-Haq Qureshi** (PAK) [4]
18. Juan Sebastian Cabal (COL) & Robert Farah (COL)
19. Mikhail Kukushkin (KAZ) & Michael Russell (USA)
(WC) 20. Daniel Cox (GBR) & James Ward (GBR)
(LL) 21. Sanchai Ratiwatana (THA) & Sonchat Ratiwatana (THA)
22. James Cerretani (USA) & Philipp Marx (GER)
23. Andreas Seppi (ITA) & Simone Vagnozzi (ITA)
24. **Daniele Bracciali** (ITA) & **Frantisek Cermak** (CZE) [16]
25. **Mark Knowles** (BAH) & **Lukasz Kubot** (POL) [10]
26. Chris Guccione (AUS) & Adil Shamasdin (CAN)
27. Carsten Ball (AUS) & Santiago Gonzalez (MEX)
28. Dustin Brown (GER) & Michael Kohlmann (GER)
29. Rainer Schuettler (GER) & Alexander Waske (GER)
30. Somdev Devvarman (IND) & Kei Nishikori (JPN)
31. Frederico Gil (POR) & Ruben Ramirez Hidalgo (ESP)
32. **Michael Llodra** (FRA) & **Nenad Zimonjic** (SRB) [6]
33. **Robert Lindstedt** (SWE) & **Horia Tecau** (ROU) [8]
(WC) 34. Chris Eaton (GBR) & Joshua Goodall (GBR)
35. Julien Benneteau (FRA) & Nicolas Mahut (FRA)
(LL) 36. Lukas Lacko (SVK) & Lukas Rosol (CZE)
37. Matthias Bachinger (GER) & Frank Moser (GER)
(WC) 38. Lleyton Hewitt (AUS) & Peter Luczak (AUS)
39. Franco Ferreiro (BRA) & Andre Sa (BRA)
40. **Juan Ignacio Chela** (ARG) & **Eduardo Schwank** (ARG) [12]
41. **Marcel Granollers** (ESP) & **Tommy Robredo** (ESP) [14]
42. Santiago Giraldo (COL) & Pere Riba (ESP)
43. Jamie Murray (GBR) & Sergiy Stakhovsky (UKR)
(Q) 44. David Rice (GBR) & Sean Thornley (GBR)
45. Arnaud Clement (FRA) & Lukas Dlouhy (CZE)
46. Robin Haase (NED) & Kenneth Skupski (GBR)
47. Ivan Dodig (CRO) & Lovro Zovko (CRO)
48. **Mahesh Bhupathi** (IND) & **Leander Paes** (IND) [3]
49. **Mariusz Fyrstenberg** (POL) & **Marcin Matkowski** (POL) [7]
50. Colin Fleming (GBR) & Ross Hutchins (GBR)
(LL) 51. Flavio Cipolla (ITA) & Paolo Lorenzi (ITA)
52. Grigor Dimitrov (BUL) & Dmitry Tursunov (RUS)
53. Ashley Fisher (AUS) & Stephen Huss (AUS)
54. Martin Damm (CZE) & Rogier Wassen (NED)
55. Filip Polasek (SVK) & Igor Zelenay (SVK)
56. **Eric Butorac** (USA) & **Jean-Julien Rojer** (AHO) [9]
57. **Marcelo Melo** (BRA) & **Bruno Soares** (BRA) [13]
58. Guillermo Garcia-Lopez (ESP) & Albert Montanes (ESP)
59. Christopher Kas (GER) & Alexander Peya (AUT)
60. Pablo Andujar (ESP) & Daniel Gimeno-Traver (ESP)
61. Kevin Anderson (RSA) & Julian Knowle (AUT)
(Q) 62. Karol Beck (SVK) & David Skoch (CZE)
(LL) 63. Leos Friedl (CZE) & David Martin (USA)
64. **Max Mirnyi** (BLR) & **Daniel Nestor** (CAN) [2]

Second Round:
Bob Bryan & Mike Bryan [1] 6/3 6/3
Alex Bogomolov Jr. & Ivo Karlovic ......7/6(2) 6/4
Simon Aspelin & Paul Hanley 6/4 6/1
Marc Lopez & David Marrero [15] ......6/3 7/6(7)
Wesley Moodie & Dick Norman [11] ......7/5 7/6(4)
Jamie Delgado & Jonathan Marray ......7/6(5) 3/6 8/6
Scott Lipsky & Rajeev Ram 4/6 6/3 6/4
Jurgen Melzer & Philipp Petzschner [5] ......6/7(4) 7/6(1) 6/4
Juan Sebastian Cabal & Robert Farah 2/6 6/2 21/19
Mikhail Kukushkin & Michael Russell 4/6 6/4 6/4
James Cerretani & Philipp Marx 6/4 6/1
Daniele Bracciali & Frantisek Cermak [16] 6/4 6/4
Chris Guccione & Adil Shamasdin ......1/6 7/6(5) 6/4
Carsten Ball & Santiago Gonzalez 5/7 6/3 13/11
Somdev Devvarman & Kei Nishikori ......6/7(3) 6/3 6/2
Michael Llodra & Nenad Zimonjic [6] 6/2 6/1
Robert Lindstedt & Horia Tecau [8] 6/2 7/5
Julien Benneteau & Nicolas Mahut ......7/6(5) 6/2
Matthias Bachinger & Frank Moser 7/5 6/4
Juan Ignacio Chela & Eduardo Schwank [12] ......6/3 7/6(5)
Marcel Granollers & Tommy Robredo ......7/6(3) 5/7 6/3
Jamie Murray & Sergiy Stakhovsky 6/3 7/5
Arnaud Clement & Lukas Dlouhy 6/4 6/2
Mahesh Bhupathi & Leander Paes [3] ......6/7(7) 6/4 6/4
Colin Fleming & Ross Hutchins 6/2 6/1
Grigor Dimitrov & Dmitry Tursunov 6/3 6/4
Ashley Fisher & Stephen Huss ......6/7(1) 7/5 9/7
Eric Butorac & Jean-Julien Rojer [9] 6/4 4/6 6/4
Marcelo Melo & Bruno Soares [13] ......7/6(3) 6/1
Christopher Kas & Alexander Peya 6/2 6/3
Kevin Anderson & Julian Knowle 7/5 6/1
Max Mirnyi & Daniel Nestor [2] 6/4 6/4

Third Round:
Bob Bryan & Mike Bryan [1] ......7/6(4) 6/4 7/5
Simon Aspelin & Paul Hanley ......6/7(4) 7/5 7/5 6/3
Wesley Moodie & Dick Norman [11] ......4/6 7/6(5) 7/6(6) 6/2
Jurgen Melzer & Philipp Petzschner [5] ......6/4 7/6(3) 4/6 6/3
Juan Sebastian Cabal & Robert Farah 6/4 6/2 6/3
James Cerretani & Philipp Marx ......4/6 7/5 7/6(5) 6/4
Carsten Ball & Santiago Gonzalez ......7/6(4) 7/6(6) 6/4
Michael Llodra & Nenad Zimonjic [6] ......6/3 6/4 7/6(5)
Robert Lindstedt & Horia Tecau [8] ......6/4 6/4 5/7 7/6(4)
Juan Ignacio Chela & Eduardo Schwank [12] ......6/2 7/6(4) 6/7(5) 6/7(6) 6/3
Marcel Granollers & Tommy Robredo [14] ......7/5 7/6(3) 6/1
Arnaud Clement & Lukas Dlouhy ......2/6 6/3 7/6(1) 6/4
Colin Fleming & Ross Hutchins ......4/6 6/2 6/7(5) 6/2 6/4
Ashley Fisher & Stephen Huss 6/4 6/3 6/3
Christopher Kas & Alexander Peya ......6/7(2) 6/1 6/4 6/2
Kevin Anderson & Julian Knowle ......7/6(2) 7/6(7) 6/3

Quarter-Finals:
Bob Bryan & Mike Bryan [1] ......6/3 4/6 6/7(5) 6/3 16/14
Jurgen Melzer & Philipp Petzschner [5] ......7/6(5) 6/3 4/6 6/2
James Cerretani & Philipp Marx ......3/6 7/6(2) 6/4 6/4
Michael Llodra & Nenad Zimonjic [6] ......6/4 7/6(9) 7/6(4)
Robert Lindstedt & Horia Tecau [8] ......7/6(6) 7/6(2) 7/6(8)
Arnaud Clement & Lukas Dlouhy 6/3 7/5 7/5
Colin Fleming & Ross Hutchins 6/3 6/4 6/2
Christopher Kas & Alexander Peya ......7/6(1) 6/4 5/7 8/6

Semi-Finals:
Bob Bryan & Mike Bryan [1] 6/3 6/4 6/4
Michael Llodra & Nenad Zimonjic [6] ......6/7(3) 7/6(7) 7/6(5) 7/5
Robert Lindstedt & Horia Tecau [8] 3/6 6/1 4/6 6/4 12/10
Christopher Kas & Alexander Peya ......6/4 6/4 6/7(2) 2/6 6/4

Final:
Bob Bryan & Mike Bryan [1] ......6/4 6/4 6/7(8) 6/7(4) 9/7
Robert Lindstedt & Horia Tecau [8] ......6/3 7/6(3) 6/2

Winner:
Bob Bryan & Mike Bryan [1] ......6/3 6/4 7/6(2)

Heavy type denotes seeded players. The figure in brackets against names denotes the order in which they have been seeded. (WC)=Wild card. (Q)=Qualifier. (LL)=Lucky loser.

EVENT III – THE LADIES' SINGLES CHAMPIONSHIP 2011
HOLDER: SERENA WILLIAMS

The Winner became the holder, for the year only, of the CHALLENGE TROPHY presented by The All England Lawn Tennis and Croquet Club in 1886. The Winner received a silver replica of the Trophy. A Silver Salver was presented to the Runner-up and a Bronze Medal to each defeated Semi-finalist. The matches were the best of three sets.

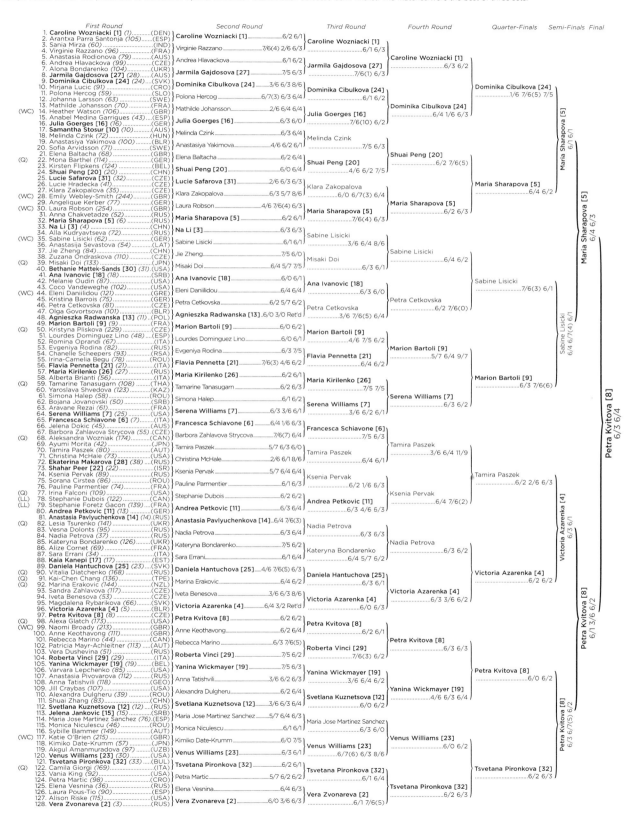

EVENT IV – THE LADIES' DOUBLES CHAMPIONSHIP 2011
HOLDERS: VANIA KING & YAROSLAVA SCHEDOVA

The Winners became the holders, for the year only, of the CHALLENGE CUPS presented by H.R.H. PRINCESS MARINA, DUCHESS OF KENT, the late President of The All England Lawn Tennis and Croquet Club in 1949 and The All England Lawn Tennis and Croquet Club in 2001. The Winners received a silver replica of the Challenge Cup. A Silver Salver was presented to each of the Runners-up and a Bronze Medal to each defeated Semi-finalist. The matches were the best of three sets.

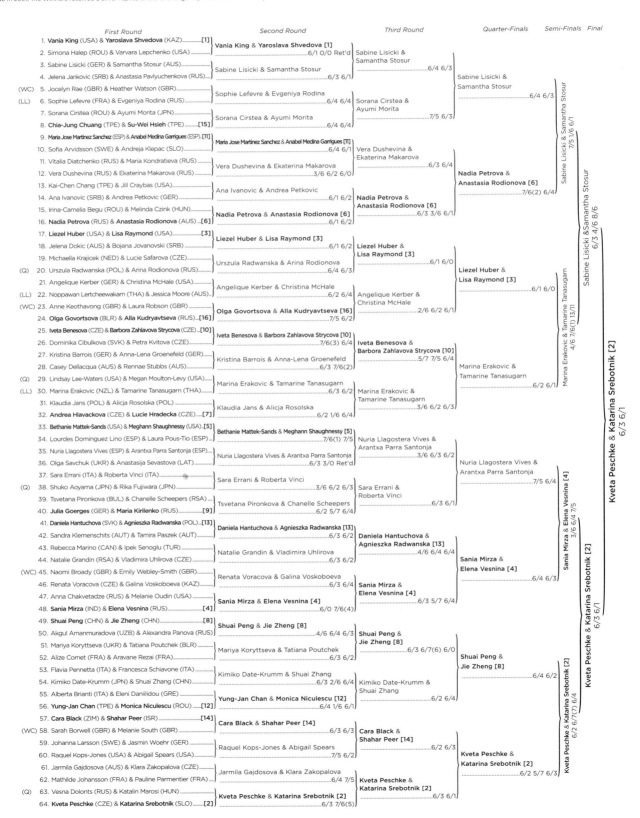

Heavy type denotes seeded players. The figure in brackets against names denotes the order in which they were seeded. (WC)=Wild card. (Q)=Qualifier. (LL)=Lucky loser.

EVENT V – THE MIXED DOUBLES CHAMPIONSHIP 2011
HOLDERS: LEANDER PAES & CARA BLACK

The Winners became the holders, for the year only, of the CHALLENGE CUPS presented by members of the family of the late Mr. S. H. SMITH in 1949 and The All England Lawn Tennis and Croquet Club in 2001.
The Winners received a silver replica of the Challenge Cup. A Silver Salver was presented to each of the Runners-up and a Bronze Medal to each defeated Semi-finalist. The matches were the best of three sets.

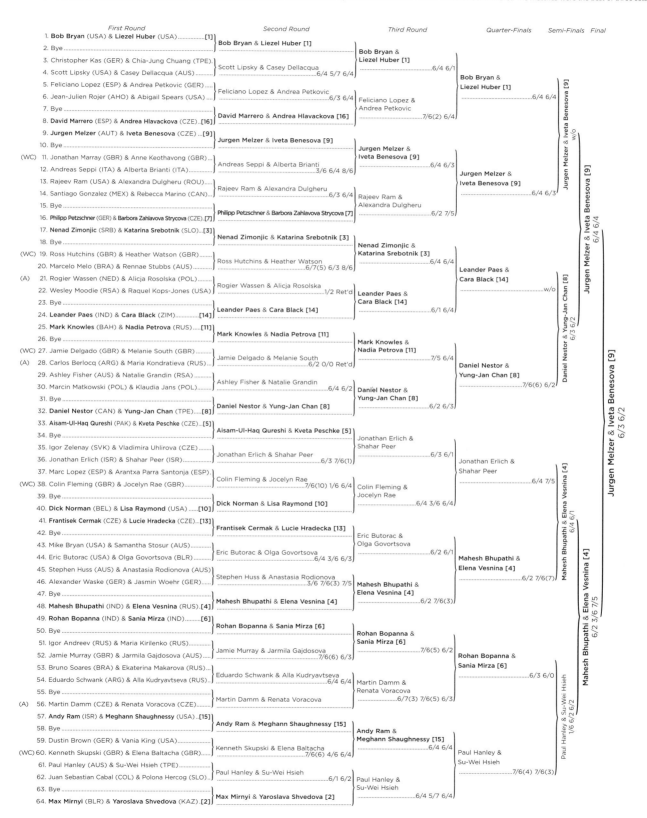

First Round

1. **Bob Bryan** (USA) & **Liezel Huber** (USA) ....[1]
2. Bye
3. Christopher Kas (GER) & Chia-Jung Chuang (TPE)
4. Scott Lipsky (USA) & Casey Dellacqua (AUS)
5. Feliciano Lopez (ESP) & Andrea Petkovic (GER)
6. Jean-Julien Rojer (AHO) & Abigail Spears (USA)
7. Bye
8. David Marrero (ESP) & **Andrea Hlavackova** (CZE)..[16]
9. **Jurgen Melzer** (AUT) & **Iveta Benesova** (CZE) ...[9]
10. Bye
(WC) 11. Jonathan Marray (GBR) & Anne Keothavong (GBR)
12. Andreas Seppi (ITA) & Alberta Brianti (ITA)
13. Rajeev Ram (USA) & Alexandra Dulgheru (ROU)
14. Santiago Gonzalez (MEX) & Rebecca Marino (CAN)
15. Bye
16. **Philipp Petzschner** (GER) & **Barbora Zahlavova Strycova** (CZE)..[7]
17. **Nenad Zimonjic** (SRB) & **Katarina Srebotnik** (SLO)..[3]
18. Bye
(WC) 19. Ross Hutchins (GBR) & Heather Watson (GBR)
20. Marcelo Melo (BRA) & Rennae Stubbs (AUS)
(A) 21. Rogier Wassen (NED) & Alicja Rosolska (POL)
22. Wesley Moodie (RSA) & Raquel Kops-Jones (USA)
23. Bye
24. **Leander Paes** (IND) & **Cara Black** (ZIM)............[14]
25. **Mark Knowles** (BAH) & **Nadia Petrova** (RUS)....[11]
26. Bye
(WC) 27. Jamie Delgado (GBR) & Melanie South (GBR)
(A) 28. Carlos Berlocq (ARG) & Maria Kondratieva (RUS)
29. Ashley Fisher (AUS) & Natalie Grandin (RSA)
30. Marcin Matkowski (POL) & Klaudia Jans (POL)
31. Bye
32. **Daniel Nestor** (CAN) & **Yung-Jan Chan** (TPE).....[8]
33. **Aisam-Ul-Haq Qureshi** (PAK) & **Kveta Peschke** (CZE)..[5]
34. Bye
35. Igor Zelenay (SVK) & Vladimira Uhlirova (CZE)
36. Jonathan Erlich (ISR) & Shahar Peer (ISR)
37. Marc Lopez (ESP) & Arantxa Parra Santonja (ESP)
(WC) 38. Colin Fleming (GBR) & Jocelyn Rae (GBR)
39. Bye
40. **Dick Norman** (BEL) & **Lisa Raymond** (USA)......[10]
41. **Frantisek Cermak** (CZE) & **Lucie Hradecka** (CZE)...[13]
42. Bye
43. Mike Bryan (USA) & Samantha Stosur (AUS)
44. Eric Butorac (USA) & Olga Govortsova (BLR)
45. Stephen Huss (AUS) & Anastasia Rodionova (AUS)
46. Alexander Waske (GER) & Jasmin Woehr (GER)
47. Bye
48. **Mahesh Bhupathi** (IND) & **Elena Vesnina** (RUS)..[4]
49. **Rohan Bopanna** (IND) & **Sania Mirza** (IND)........[6]
50. Bye
51. Igor Andreev (RUS) & Maria Kirilenko (RUS)
52. Jamie Murray (GBR) & Jarmila Gajdosova (AUS)
53. Bruno Soares (BRA) & Ekaterina Makarova (RUS)
54. Eduardo Schwank (ARG) & Alla Kudryavtseva (RUS)
55. Bye
(A) 56. Martin Damm (CZE) & Renata Voracova (CZE)
57. **Andy Ram** (ISR) & **Meghann Shaughnessy** (USA)..[15]
58. Bye
59. Dustin Brown (GER) & Vania King (USA)
(WC) 60. Kenneth Skupski (GBR) & Elena Baltacha (GBR)
61. Paul Hanley (AUS) & Su-Wei Hsieh (TPE)
62. Juan Sebastian Cabal (COL) & Polona Hercog (SLO)
63. Bye
64. **Max Mirnyi** (BLR) & **Yaroslava Shvedova** (KAZ)..[2]

Second Round

Bob Bryan & Liezel Huber [1]
Scott Lipsky & Casey Dellacqua 6/4 5/7 6/4
Feliciano Lopez & Andrea Petkovic 6/3 6/4
David Marrero & Andrea Hlavackova [16]
Jurgen Melzer & Iveta Benesova [9]
Andreas Seppi & Alberta Brianti 3/6 6/4 8/6
Rajeev Ram & Alexandra Dulgheru 6/3 6/4
Philipp Petzschner & **Barbora Zahlavova Strycova** [7]
Nenad Zimonjic & Katarina Srebotnik [3]
Ross Hutchins & Heather Watson .... 6/7(5) 6/3 8/6
Rogier Wassen & Alicja Rosolska .... 1/2 Ret'd
Leander Paes & **Cara Black** [14]
Mark Knowles & Nadia Petrova [11]
Jamie Delgado & Melanie South .... 6/2 0/0 Ret'd
Ashley Fisher & Natalie Grandin 6/4 6/2
Daniel Nestor & **Yung-Jan Chan** [8]
Aisam-Ul-Haq Qureshi & Kveta Peschke [5]
Jonathan Erlich & Shahar Peer .... 6/3 7/6(1)
Colin Fleming & Jocelyn Rae .... 7/6(10) 1/6 6/4
Dick Norman & **Lisa Raymond** [10]
Frantisek Cermak & Lucie Hradecka [13]
Eric Butorac & Olga Govortsova 6/4 3/6 6/3
Stephen Huss & Anastasia Rodionova .... 3/6 7/6(3) 7/5
Mahesh Bhupathi & **Elena Vesnina** [4]
Rohan Bopanna & Sania Mirza [6]
Jamie Murray & Jarmila Gajdosova .... 7/6(6) 6/3
Eduardo Schwank & Alla Kudryavtseva 6/4 6/4
Martin Damm & Renata Voracova
Andy Ram & Meghann Shaughnessy [15]
Kenneth Skupski & Elena Baltacha .... 7/6(6) 4/6 6/4
Paul Hanley & Su-Wei Hsieh 6/1 6/2
Max Mirnyi & **Yaroslava Shvedova** [2]

Third Round

Bob Bryan & Liezel Huber [1] 6/4 6/1
Feliciano Lopez & Andrea Petkovic .... 7/6(2) 6/4
Jurgen Melzer & Iveta Benesova [9] 6/4 6/3
Rajeev Ram & Alexandra Dulgheru 6/2 7/5
Nenad Zimonjic & Katarina Srebotnik [3] 6/4 6/4
Leander Paes & Cara Black [14] 6/1 6/4
Mark Knowles & Nadia Petrova [11] 7/5 6/4
Daniel Nestor & Yung-Jan Chan [8] 6/2 6/3
Jonathan Erlich & Shahar Peer 6/3 6/1
Colin Fleming & Jocelyn Rae 6/4 3/6 6/4
Eric Butorac & Olga Govortsova 6/2 6/1
Mahesh Bhupathi & Elena Vesnina [4] .... 6/2 7/6(3)
Rohan Bopanna & Sania Mirza [6] .... 7/6(5) 6/2
Martin Damm & Renata Voracova .... 6/7(3) 7/6(5) 6/3
Andy Ram & Meghann Shaughnessy [15] 6/4 6/4
Paul Hanley & Su-Wei Hsieh 6/4 5/7 6/4

Quarter-Finals

Bob Bryan & Liezel Huber [1] 6/4 6/4
Jurgen Melzer & Iveta Benesova [9] 6/4 6/3
Leander Paes & Cara Black [14] .... w/o
Daniel Nestor & Yung-Jan Chan [8] .... 7/6(6) 6/2
Jonathan Erlich & Shahar Peer 6/4 7/5
Mahesh Bhupathi & Elena Vesnina [4] .... 6/2 7/6(7)
Rohan Bopanna & Sania Mirza [6] 6/3 6/0
Paul Hanley & Su-Wei Hsieh .... 7/6(4) 7/6(3)

Semi-Finals

Jurgen Melzer & Iveta Benesova [9] .... w/o
Daniel Nestor & Yung-Jan Chan [8] 6/3 6/2
Mahesh Bhupathi & Elena Vesnina [4] 6/4 6/1
Paul Hanley & Su-Wei Hsieh 1/6 6/2 6/2

Final

Jurgen Melzer & Iveta Benesova [9] 6/4 6/4
Mahesh Bhupathi & Elena Vesnina [4] 6/2 3/6 7/5

Jurgen Melzer & Iveta Benesova [9] 6/3 6/2

Heavy type denotes seeded players. The figure in brackets against names denotes the order in which they were seeded. (WC)=Wild card. (A)=Alternates.

EVENT VI – THE GENTLEMEN'S INVITATION DOUBLES 2011
HOLDERS: DONALD JOHNSON & JARED PALMER

The Winners became the holders, for the year only, of a cup presented by The All England Lawn Tennis and Croquet Club. The Winners received miniature silver salvers. A silver medal was presented to each of the Runners-up. The matches were the best of three sets. If a match reached one set all a 10 point tie-break replaced the third set.

GROUP A	Jonas Bjorkman (SWE) & Todd Woodbridge (AUS)	Barry Cowan (GBR) & Cedric Pioline (FRA)	Goran Ivanisevic (CRO) & Richard Krajicek (NED)	Donald Johnson (USA) & Jared Palmer (USA)	WINS	LOSSES	FINAL
Jonas Bjorkman (SWE) & Todd Woodbridge (AUS)		6/3 6/4 W	6/3 6/4 W	3/6 7/6(2) [10/4] W	3	0	
Barry Cowan (GBR) & Cedric Pioline (FRA)	3/6 4/6 L		4/6 4/6 L	6/3 6/7(2) [4/10] L	0	3	Jonas Bjorkman & Todd Woodbridge
Goran Ivanisevic (CRO) & Richard Krajicek (NED)	3/6 4/6 L	6/4 6/4 W		5/7 6/7(2) L	1	2	
Donald Johnson (USA) & Jared Palmer (USA)	6/3 6/7(2) [4/10] L	3/6 7/6(2) [10/4] W	7/5 7/6(2) W		2	1	

GROUP B	Jacco Eltingh (NED) & Paul Haarhuis (NED)	Wayne Ferreira (RSA) & Yevgeny Kafelnikov (RUS)	Justin Gimelstob (USA) & Todd Martin (USA)	Mark Petchey (GBR) & Chris Wilkinson (GBR)	WINS	LOSSES
Jacco Eltingh (NED) & Paul Haarhuis (NED)		6/3 3/6 [8/10] L	6/4 7/6(2) W	6/3 6/4 W	2	1
Wayne Ferreira (RSA) & Yevgeny Kafelnikov (RUS)	3/6 6/3 [10/8] W		3/6 6/3 [11/13] L	7/5 6/3 W	2	1
Justin Gimelstob (USA) & Todd Martin (USA)	4/6 6/7(2) L	6/3 3/6 [13/11] W		6/3 7/6(0) W	2	1
Mark Petchey (GBR) & Chris Wilkinson (GBR)	3/6 4/6 L	5/7 3/6 L	3/6 6/7(0) L		0	3

Final group B: Jacco Eltingh & Paul Haarhuis

Overall Final: Jacco Eltingh & Paul Haarhuis 3/6 6/3 [13/11]

This event was played on a 'round robin' basis. 8 invited pairs were divided into 2 groups and each pair in each group played one another.
The pairs winning most matches were the winners of their respective groups and played a final round as indicated above.
If matches were equal in any group, the head to head result between the two pairs with the same number of wins, determined the winning pair of the group.
If that did not split the ties, then the percentage of sets won to sets played decided.

EVENT VII – THE GENTLEMEN'S SENIOR INVITATION DOUBLES 2011
HOLDERS: PAT CASH & MARK WOODFORDE

The Winners became the holders, for the year only, of a Cup presented by The All England Lawn Tennis and Croquet Club. The Winners received miniature silver salvers. A Silver Medal was presented to each of the Runners-up. The matches were the best of three sets. If a match reached one set all a 10 point tie-break replaced the third set.

GROUP A	Mansour Bahrami (IRI) & Andrew Castle (GBR)	Pat Cash (AUS) & Mark Woodforde (AUS)	Kevin Curren (USA) & Johan Kriek (USA)	Darren Cahill (AUS) & Mikael Pernfors (SWE)	WINS	LOSSES	FINAL
Mansour Bahrami (IRI) & Andrew Castle (GBR)		3/6 5/7 L	6/4 3/6 [6/10] L	Walk Over W	1	2	
Pat Cash (AUS) & Mark Woodforde (AUS)	6/3 7/5 W		4/6 6/3 [10/5] W	2/1 Ret'd W	3	0	Pat Cash & Mark Woodforde
Kevin Curren (USA) & Johan Kriek (USA)	4/6 6/3 [10/6] W	6/4 3/6 [5/10] L		Walk Over W	2	1	
Darren Cahill (AUS) & Mikael Pernfors (SWE)	Walked Over L	1/2 Ret'd L	Walked Over L		0	3	

GROUP B	Vijay Amritraj (IND) & John Fitzgerald (AUS)	Jeremy Bates (GBR) & Anders Jarryd (SWE)	Peter Fleming (USA) & Brad Gilbert (USA)	Peter McNamara (AUS) & Paul McNamee (AUS)	WINS	LOSSES
Vijay Amritraj (IND) & John Fitzgerald (AUS)		2/6 2/6 L	7/6(5) 6/7(4) [10/8] W	6/2 6/2 W	2	1
Jeremy Bates (GBR) & Anders Jarryd (SWE)	6/2 6/2 W		6/4 6/3 W	6/2 6/4 W	3	0
Peter Fleming (USA) & Brad Gilbert (USA)	6/7(5) 7/6(4) [8/10] L	4/6 3/6 L		6/3 6/7(2) [9/11] L	0	3
Peter McNamara (AUS) & Paul McNamee (AUS)	2/6 2/6 L	2/6 4/6 L	3/6 7/6(2) [11/9] W		1	2

Final group B: Jeremy Bates & Anders Jarryd

Overall Final: Pat Cash & Mark Woodforde 6/3 5/7 [10/5]

This event was played on a 'round robin' basis. 8 invited pairs were divided into 2 groups and each pair in each group played one another.
The pairs winning most matches were the winners of their respective groups and played a final round as indicated above.
If matches were equal in any group, the head to head result between the two pairs with the same number of wins, determined the winning pair of the group.
If that did not split the ties, then the percentage of sets won to sets played decided.

ALPHABETICAL LIST – INVITATION DOUBLES EVENTS

GENTLEMEN

Cash P. (Australia)
Eltingh J. (Netherlands)
Ferreira W. (South Africa)
Forget G. (France)

Haarhuis P. (Netherlands)
Jensen L. (USA)
Jensen M. (USA)
Johnson D. (USA)

Middleton T.J. (USA)
Palmer J. (USA)
Petchey M. (Great Britain)
Pioline C. (France)

Wheaton D. (USA)
Wilkinson C. (Great Britain)
Woodbridge T.A. (Australia)
Woodforde M. (Australia)

LADIES

Appelmans Miss S. (Belgium)
Bassett-Seguso Mrs C. (Canada)
Bollegraf Miss M.M. (Netherlands)
Croft Miss A. (Great Britain)

Durie Miss J.M. (Great Britain)
Kloss Miss I. (South Africa)
Magers Mrs G. (USA)
Mandlikova Miss H. (Australia)

Martinez Miss C. (Spain)
Navratilova Miss M. (USA)
Nideffer Mrs R.D. (USA)
Novotna Miss J. (Czech Republic)

Rinaldi Mrs K. (USA)
Smylie Mrs E.M. (Australia)
Sukova Miss H. (Czech Republic)
Tauziat Miss N. (France)

EVENT VIII – THE LADIES' INVITATION DOUBLES 2011
HOLDERS: MARTINA NAVRATILOVA & JANA NOVOTNA

The Winners became the holders, for the year only, of a Cup presented by The All England Lawn Tennis and Croquet Club. The Winners received miniature Cups. A Silver Medal was presented to each of the Runners-up. The matches were the best of three sets. If a match reached one set all a 10 point tie-break replaced the third set.

GROUP A	Annabel Croft (GBR) & Samantha Smith (GBR)	Conchita Martinez (ESP) & Nathalie Tauziat (FRA)	Martina Navratilova (USA) & Jana Novotna (CZE)	Helena Sukova (CZE) & Andrea Temesvari (HUN)	WINS	LOSSES	FINAL
Annabel Croft (GBR) & Samantha Smith (GBR)		0/6 3/6 L	0/6 3/6 L	0/6 3/6 L	0	3	
Conchita Martinez (ESP) & Nathalie Tauziat (FRA)	6/0 6/3 W		4/6 2/6 L	6/2 7/5 W	2	1	
Martina Navratilova (USA) & Jana Novotna (CZE)	6/0 6/3 W	6/4 6/2 W		7/6(4) 6/2 W	3	0	Martina Navratilova & Jana Novotna
Helena Sukova (CZE) & Andrea Temesvari (HUN)	6/0 6/3 W	2/6 5/7 L	6/7(4) 2/6 L		1	2	

GROUP B	Tracy Austin (USA) & Kathy Rinaldi (USA)	Lindsay Davenport (USA) & Martina Hingis (SUI)	Gigi Fernandez (USA) & Natasha Zvereva (BLR)	Magdalena Maleeva (BUL) & Barbara Schett (AUT)	WINS	LOSSES	FINAL
Tracy Austin (USA) & Kathy Rinaldi (USA)		2/6 3/6 L	3/6 7/5 [9/11] L	3/6 4/6 L	0	3	
Lindsay Davenport (USA) & Martina Hingis (SUI)	6/2 6/3 W		6/2 6/2 W	6/1 6/1 W	3	0	Lindsay Davenport & Martina Hingis
Gigi Fernandez (USA) & Natasha Zvereva (BLR)	6/3 5/7 [11/9] W	2/6 2/6 L		1/6 1/6 L	1	2	
Magdalena Maleeva (BUL) & Barbara Schett (AUT)	6/3 6/4 W	1/6 1/6 L	6/1 6/1 W		2	1	

FINAL: Lindsay Davenport & Martina Hingis — Martina Navratilova & Jana Novotna 6/4 6/4

EVENT IX – THE WHEELCHAIR GENTLEMEN'S DOUBLES 2011
HOLDERS: ROBIN AMMERLAAN & STEFAN OLSSON

The Winners received Silver Salvers. The matches were the best of three tie-break sets.

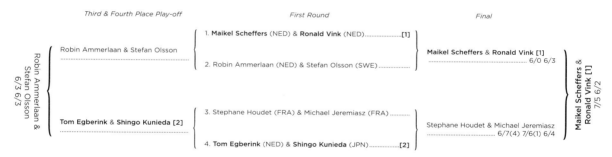

Third & Fourth Place Play-off

Robin Ammerlaan & Stefan Olsson 6/3 6/3

Robin Ammerlaan & Stefan Olsson
Tom Egberink & Shingo Kunieda [2]

First Round

1. **Maikel Scheffers** (NED) & **Ronald Vink** (NED) .... [1]
2. Robin Ammerlaan (NED) & Stefan Olsson (SWE) ....
3. Stephane Houdet (FRA) & Michael Jeremiasz (FRA) ....
4. **Tom Egberink** (NED) & **Shingo Kunieda** (JPN) .... [2]

Final

Maikel Scheffers & Ronald Vink [1] 6/0 6/3
Stephane Houdet & Michael Jeremiasz .... 6/7(4) 7/6(1) 6/4

Maikel Scheffers & Ronald Vink [1] 7/5 6/2

EVENT X – THE WHEELCHAIR LADIES' DOUBLES 2011
HOLDERS: ESTHER VERGEER & SHARON WALRAVEN

The Winners received Silver Salvers. The matches were the best of three tie-break sets.

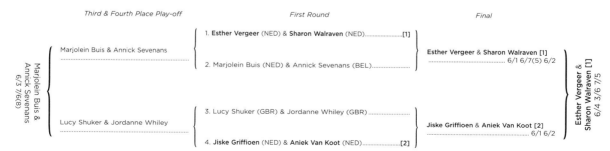

Third & Fourth Place Play-off

Marjolein Buis & Annick Sevenans 6/3 7/6(8)

Marjolein Buis & Annick Sevenans
Lucy Shuker & Jordanne Whiley

First Round

1. **Esther Vergeer** (NED) & **Sharon Walraven** (NED) .... [1]
2. Marjolein Buis (NED) & Annick Sevenans (BEL) ....
3. Lucy Shuker (GBR) & Jordanne Whiley (GBR) ....
4. **Jiske Griffioen** (NED) & **Aniek Van Koot** (NED) .... [2]

Final

Esther Vergeer & Sharon Walraven [1] .... 6/1 6/7(5) 6/2
Jiske Griffioen & Aniek Van Koot [2] 6/1 6/2

Esther Vergeer & Sharon Walraven [1] 6/4 3/6 7/5

ALPHABETICAL LIST – GENTLEMEN'S SENIOR INVITATION DOUBLES EVENT

Amritraj V. (India)
Bahrami M. (Iran)
Bates M.J. (Great Britain)
Curren K. (USA)
Fitzgerald J.B. (Australia)

Flach K. (USA)
Fleming P. (USA)
Guenthardt H. (Switzerland)
Jarryd A. (Sweden)
Leconte H. (France)

Mayer G. (USA)
McNamara P. (Australia)
McNamee P.F. (Australia)
Seguso R. (USA)
Taroczy B. (Hungary)

Vilas G. (Argentina)

EVENT XI – THE BOYS' SINGLES CHAMPIONSHIP 2011

HOLDER: MARTON FUCSOVICS

The Winner became the holder, for the year only, of a Cup presented by The All England Lawn Tennis and Croquet Club. The Winner received a miniature Cup and the Runner-up received a memento. The matches were best of three sets.

First Round

1. **Jiri Vesely [1]** *(1)*....(CZE)
(WC) 2. Jonathan Cornish *(185)*....(GBR)
3. Bruno Sant'anna *(21)*....(BRA)
4. Alexios Halebian *(38)*....(USA)
5. Mathias Bourgue *(44)*....(FRA)
6. Filip Peliwo *(46)*....(CAN)
(Q) 7. Nick Kyrgios *(81)*....(AUS)
8. **Liam Broady [15]** *(16)*....(GBR)
9. **Andrew Whittington [9]** *(9)*....(AUS)
(WC) 10. Luke Bambridge *(90)*....(GBR)
(Q) 11. Robin Kern *(36)*....(GER)
12. Jannick Lupescu *(52)*....(NED)
13. Yaraslau Shyla *(32)*....(BLR)
14. Vladyslav Manafov *(26)*....(UKR)
(Q) 15. Oriol Roca Batalla *(42)*....(ESP)
16. **Filip Horansky [5]** *(6)*....(SVK)
17. **Oliver Golding [4]** *(5)*....(GBR)
18. Aslan Karatsev *(77)*....(RUS)
(WC) 19. Jason Kubler *(618)*....(AUS)
20. Mate Delic *(23)*....(CRO)
21. Pedja Krstin *(33)*....(SRB)
22. Marco Aurei Nunez *(47)*....(MEX)
23. Marcos Giron *(31)*....(USA)
24. **Andres Artunedo Martinavarr [14]** *(15)*....(ESP)
25. **Joao Pedro Sorgi [11]** *(12)*....(BRA)
26. Kyle Edmund *(35)*....(GBR)
27. Mac Styslinger *(34)*....(USA)
28. Julien Cagnina *(27)*....(BEL)
(WC) 29. Joshua Ward-Hibbert *(168)*....(GBR)
30. Maxim Dubarenco *(19)*....(MDA)
31. Diego Hidalgo *(20)*....(ECU)
32. **Dominic Thiem [7]** *(7)*....(AUT)
33. **Mate Pavic [8]** *(8)*....(CRO)
34. Mitchell Krueger *(28)*....(USA)
(Q) 35. Axel Alvarez Llamas *(65)*....(ESP)
(WC) 36. Evan Hoyt *(180)*....(GBR)
37. Matias Sborowitz *(25)*....(CHI)
(Q) 38. Hassan Ndayishimiye *(112)*....(BDI)
39. Frederico Ferreira Silva *(48)*....(POR)
40. **Patrick Ofner [12]** *(13)*....(AUT)
41. **Jeson Patrombon [13]** *(14)*....(PHI)
42. Julian Lenz *(40)*....(GER)
(WC) 43. Toby Martin *(297)*....(GBR)
44. Kimmer Coppejans *(39)*....(BEL)
45. Ben Wagland *(30)*....(AUS)
46. Shane Vinsant *(24)*....(USA)
47. Kaichi Uchida *(37)*....(JPN)
48. **Hugo Dellien [3]** *(4)*....(BOL)
49. **Roberto Carballes Baena [6]** *(11)*(ESP)
(WC) 50. Andrew Bettles *(4999)*....(GBR)
51. Nikola Milojevic *(22)*....(SRB)
52. Joris De Loore *(18)*....(BEL)
53. Sean Berman *(29)*....(USA)
(Q) 54. Enzo Couacaud *(50)*....(FRA)
55. Teodor Nicolae Marin *(53)*....(ROU)
56. **George Morgan [10]** *(10)*....(GBR)
57. **Luke Saville [16]** *(17)*....(AUS)
58. Lukas Vrnak *(54)*....(CZE)
59. Evgeny Karlovskiy *(68)*....(RUS)
(Q) 60. Dennis Novikov *(51)*....(USA)
61. Wayne Montgomery *(43)*....(RSA)
(WC) 62. Oliver Hudson *(4999)*....(GBR)
(Q) 63. Dennis Novak *(59)*....(AUT)
64. **Thiago Moura Monteiro [2]** *(3)*..(BRA)

Second Round

Jiri Vesely [1]....6/4 6/2
Alexios Halebian....6/4 6/4
Mathias Bourgue....7/5 6/1
Liam Broady [15]....6/3 6/7(3) 6/2
Andrew Whittington [9]....7/6(4) 6/3
Robin Kern....6/1 6/2
Yaraslau Shyla....4/6 7/6(5) 6/3
Filip Horansky [5]....6/4 7/6(3)
Oliver Golding [4]....4/6 7/6(3) 6/4
Jason Kubler....4/6 6/4 10/8
Pedja Krstin....6/4 5/7 6/4
Marcos Giron....6/2 7/5
Kyle Edmund....6/3 6/3
Julien Cagnina....7/6(4) 6/3
Joshua Ward-Hibbert....7/5 6/4
Dominic Thiem [7]....6/2 6/1
Mate Pavic [8]....3/6 7/6(5) 8/6
Evan Hoyt....6/3 6/4
Hassan Ndayishimiye....6/4 6/4
Frederico Ferreira Silva....3/6 6/3 6/2
Jeson Patrombon [13]....2/6 6/4 6/4
Kimmer Coppejans....6/4 6/4
Ben Wagland....6/3 4/6 8/6
Kaichi Uchida....7/6(4) 6/1
Roberto Carballes Baena [6]....6/3 6/4
Joris De Loore....6/2 6/4
Sean Berman....7/6(4) 6/2
George Morgan [10]....6/4 4/6 6/1
Luke Saville [16]....6/1 6/2
Evgeny Karlovskiy....7/5 6/4
Oliver Hudson....6/4 3/6 7/5
Thiago Moura Monteiro [2]6/3 1/6 15/13

Third Round

Jiri Vesely [1]....6/4 6/4
Liam Broady [15]....6/1 6/4
Robin Kern....6/4 6/4
Filip Horansky [5]....6/4 6/4
Jason Kubler....7/6(7) 6/2
Marcos Giron....6/4 6/2
Julien Cagnina....3/6 7/6(6) 6/4
Dominic Thiem [7]....6/2 7/5
Mate Pavic [8]....7/6(3) 6/2
Frederico Ferreira Silva....4/6 7/5 6/4
Kimmer Coppejans....7/6(1) 6/1
Kaichi Uchida....7/6(3) 4/6 6/3
Joris De Loore....1/6 6/4 6/4
Sean Berman....6/3 6/4
Luke Saville [16]....7/5 7/6(7)
Thiago Moura Monteiro [2]....6/4 3/6 6/3

Quarter-Finals

Liam Broady [15]....6/4 7/5
Robin Kern....6/3 6/1
Jason Kubler....6/3 6/3
Julien Cagnina....6/4 6/2
Mate Pavic [8]....4/6 6/4 6/3
Kaichi Uchida....6/3 7/5
Joris De Loore....6/4 7/6(3)
Luke Saville [16]....7/6(8) 6/3

Semi-Finals

Liam Broady [15]....7/6(4) 4/6 13/11
Jason Kubler....6/3 6/1
Kaichi Uchida....4/6 7/6(7) 10/8
Luke Saville [16]....6/7(1) 6/2 6/2

Final

Liam Broady [15] 6/4 6/3
Luke Saville [16] 6/4 6/1

Luke Saville [16] 2/6 6/4 6/2

Heavy type denotes seeded players. The figure in brackets against names denotes the order in which they were seeded.
(WC)=Wild card. (Q)=Qualifier.

EVENT XII – THE BOYS' DOUBLES CHAMPIONSHIP 2011

HOLDERS: LIAM BROADY & TOM FARQUHARSON

The Winners became the holders, for the year only, of a Cup presented by The All England Lawn Tennis and Croquet Club.
The Winners received miniature Cups and the Runners-up received mementos. The matches were best of three sets.

First Round

1. **Oliver Golding** (GBR) & **Jiri Vesely** (CZE)....[1]
(WC) 2. Andrew Bettles (GBR) & Toby Martin (GBR)....
3. Marcos Giron (USA) & Alexios Halebian (USA)....
4. Robin Kern (GER) & Julian Lenz (GER)....
5. Kimmer Coppejans (BEL) & Filip Peliwo (CAN)....
6. Julien Cagnina (BEL) & Joris De Loore (BEL)....
7. Maxim Dubarenco (MDA) & Vladyslav Manafov (UKR)..
8. **Luke Saville** (AUS) & **Joao Pedro Sorgi** (BRA)..[7]
9. **Andres Artunedo Martinavarr** (ESP) & **Roberto Carballes Baena** (ESP)..[3]
10. Mitchell Krueger (USA) & Shane Vinsant (USA)....
11. Mathias Bourgue (FRA) & Enzo Couacaud (FRA)...
12. Dennis Novak (AUT) & Lukas Vrnak (CZE)....
(WC) 13. Sam Hutt (GBR) & Joshua Ward-Hibbert (GBR)....
14. Aslan Karatsev (RUS) & Evgeny Karlovskiy (RUS)..
15. Pedja Krstin (SRB) & Jannick Lupescu (NED)....
16. **Hugo Dellien** (BOL) & **Diego Hidalgo** (ECU)....[6]
17. **Thiago Moura Monteiro** (BRA) & **Bruno Sant'anna** (BRA)..[5]
(WC) 18. Luke Bambridge (GBR) & Kyle Edmund (GBR)....
19. Jaden Grinter (NZL) & Jeson Patrombon (PHI)....
20. Ben Wagland (AUS) & Andrew Whittington (AUS)
21. Connor Farren (USA) & Mac Styslinger (USA)....
(A) 22. Hassan Ndayishimiye (BDI) & Benjamin Ugarte (CHI)..
23. Dennis Novikov (USA) & Kaichi Uchida (JPN)....
24. **Liam Broady** (GBR) & **Filip Horansky** (SVK)....[4]
25. **Mate Delic** (CRO) & **Dominic Thiem** (AUT)....[8]
26. Axel Alvarez Llamas (ESP) & Oriol Roca Batalla (ESP)..
27. Marco Aurei Nunez (MEX) & Yaraslau Shyla (BLR).
(WC) 28. Jonathan Cornish (GBR) & Evan Hoyt (GBR)....
29. Matias Sborowitz (CHI) & Frederico Ferreira Silva (POR)...
30. Stefan Lindmark (SWE) & Nikola Milojevic (SRB)....
31. Sean Berman (USA) & Nick Kyrgios (AUS)....
32. **George Morgan** (GBR) & **Mate Pavic** (CRO)....[2]

Second Round

Oliver Golding & **Jiri Vesely [1]**....7/5 6/3
Robin Kern & Julian Lenz....6/4 7/6(7)
Julien Cagnina & Joris De Loore....6/4 6/2
Maxim Dubarenco & Vladyslav Manafov ...7/6(1) 6/7(4) 6/1
Andres Artunedo Martinavarr & **Roberto Carballes Baena [3]**..6/0 6/7(3) 6/2
Dennis Novak & Lukas Vrnak....6/1 6/1
Sam Hutt & Joshua Ward-Hibbert....4/6 7/5 6/3
Hugo Dellien & **Diego Hidalgo [6]**....6/2 7/6(5)
Luke Bambridge & Kyle Edmund....6/4 5/7 11/9
Ben Wagland & Andrew Whittington ..6/3 6/7(5) 6/3
Connor Farren & Mac Styslinger....6/1 6/4
Liam Broady & **Filip Horansky [4]**....4/6 6/4 6/1
Axel Alvarez Llamas & Oriol Roca Batalla ..6/4 7/6(1)
Marco Aurei Nunez & Yaraslau Shyla ..7/6(3) 4/6 6/4
Stefan Lindmark & Nikola Milojevic....7/6(3) 6/4
George Morgan & **Mate Pavic [2]**....6/7(1) 6/1 6/4

Quarter-Finals

Oliver Golding & **Jiri Vesely [1]**....6/3 6/3
Maxim Dubarenco & Vladyslav Manafov....6/3 7/6(6)
Andres Artunedo Martinavarr & **Roberto Carballes Baena [3]**....6/4 6/1
Sam Hutt & Joshua Ward-Hibbert....6/3 7/6(5)
Ben Wagland & Andrew Whittington....7/5 6/2
Liam Broady & **Filip Horansky [4]**....6/2 3/6 6/4
Axel Alvarez Llamas & Oriol Roca Batalla....7/6(3) 7/5
George Morgan & **Mate Pavic [2]**....7/6(7) 7/6(5)

Semi-Finals

Oliver Golding & **Jiri Vesely [1]**....7/6(5) 6/3
Andres Artunedo Martinavarr & **Roberto Carballes Baena [3]**....6/3 6/2
Liam Broady & **Filip Horansky [4]**....6/3 6/3
George Morgan & **Mate Pavic [2]**....6/4 6/2

Final

Oliver Golding & **Jiri Vesely [1]** 7/5 7/6(5)
George Morgan & **Mate Pavic [2]** 6/3 7/6(2)

George Morgan & **Mate Pavic [2]** 3/6 6/4 7/5

Heavy type denotes seeded players. The figure in brackets against names denotes the order in which they were seeded.
(WC)=Wild card. (A)=Alternates

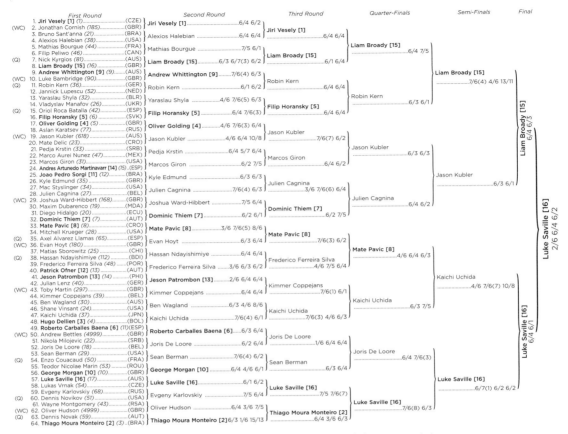

EVENT XIII – THE GIRLS' SINGLES CHAMPIONSHIP 2011
HOLDER: KRISTYANA PLISKOVA

The Winner became the holder, for the year only, of a Cup presented by The All England Lawn Tennis and Croquet Club.
The Winner received a miniature Cup and the Runner-up received a memento. The matches were best of three sets.

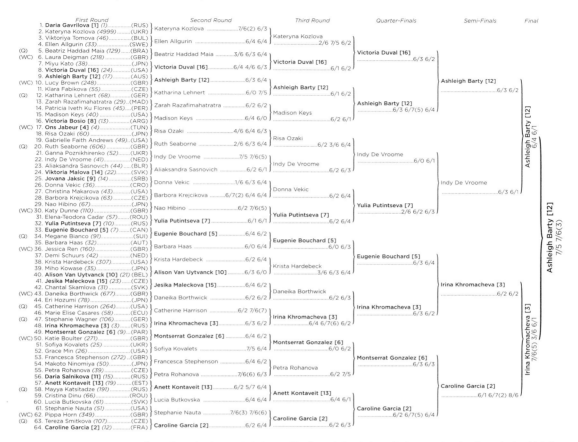

First Round	Second Round	Third Round	Quarter-Finals	Semi-Finals	Final

First Round:
1. Daria Gavrilova [1] (1) (RUS)
2. Kateryna Kozlova (4999) (UKR)
3. Viktoriya Tomova (46) (BUL)
4. Ellen Allgurin (33) (SWE)
(Q) 5. Beatriz Haddad Maia (129) (BRA)
(WC) 6. Laura Deigman (218) (GBR)
7. Miyu Kato (38) (JPN)
8. Victoria Duval [16] (24) (USA)
9. Ashleigh Barty [12] (17) (AUS)
(WC) 10. Lucy Brown (248) (GBR)
11. Klara Fabikova (55) (CZE)
12. Katharina Lehnert (68) (GER)
(Q) 13. Zarah Razafimahatratra (29) (MAD)
14. Patricia Iveth Ku Flores (45) (PER)
15. Madison Keys (40) (USA)
16. Victoria Bosio [8] (13) (ARG)
(WC) 17. Ons Jabeur [4] (4) (TUN)
18. Risa Ozaki (60) (JPN)
19. Gabrielle Faith Andrews (49) (USA)
(Q) 20. Ruth Seaborne (606) (GBR)
21. Ganna Poznikhirenko (52) (UKR)
22. Indy De Vroome (41) (NED)
23. Aliaksandra Sasnovich (44) (BLR)
24. Viktoria Malova (14) (22) (SVK)
25. Jovana Jaksic [9] (14) (SRB)
26. Donna Vekic (36) (CRO)
27. Christina Makarova (43) (USA)
28. Barbora Krejcikova (63) (CZE)
29. Nao Hibino (67) (JPN)
(WC) 30. Katy Dunne (110) (GBR)
31. Elena-Teodora Cadar (57) (ROU)
32. Yulia Putintseva [7] (10) (RUS)
33. Eugenie Bouchard [5] (7) (CAN)
(Q) 34. Megane Bianco (91) (SUI)
35. Barbara Haas (32) (AUT)
(WC) 36. Jessica Ren (160) (GBR)
37. Demi Schuurs (42) (NED)
38. Krista Hardebeck (307) (USA)
39. Miho Kowase (35) (JPN)
40. Alison Van Uytvanck [10] (21) (BEL)
41. Jesika Maleckova [15] (23) (CZE)
42. Chantal Skamlova (31) (SVK)
(WC) 43. Daneika Borthwick (677) (GBR)
44. Eri Hozumi (78) (JPN)
(Q) 45. Catherine Harrison (264) (USA)
46. Marie Elise Casares (58) (ECU)
(Q) 47. Stephanie Wagner (106) (GER)
48. Irina Khromacheva [3] (3) (RUS)
49. Montserrat Gonzalez [6] (9) (PAR)
(WC) 50. Katie Boulter (271) (GBR)
51. Sofiya Kovalets (25) (UKR)
52. Grace Min (26) (USA)
53. Francesca Stephenson (272) (GBR)
54. Makoto Ninomiya (50) (JPN)
55. Petra Rohanova (39) (CZE)
56. Daria Salnikova [11] (15) (RUS)
57. Anett Kontaveit [13] (19) (EST)
58. Mayya Katsitadze (191) (RUS)
(Q) 59. Cristina Dinu (66) (ROU)
60. Lucia Butkovska (61) (SVK)
61. Stephanie Nauta (51) (USA)
(WC) 62. Pippa Horn (349) (GBR)
(Q) 63. Tereza Smitkova (107) (CZE)
64. Caroline Garcia [2] (12) (FRA)

Second Round:
Kateryna Kozlova 7/6(2) 6/3
Ellen Allgurin 6/4 6/3
Beatriz Haddad Maia 3/6 6/3 6/4
Victoria Duval [16] 6/4 4/6 6/3
Ashleigh Barty [12] 6/3 6/4
Katharina Lehnert 6/0 7/5
Zarah Razafimahatratra 6/2 6/2
Madison Keys 6/4 6/0
Risa Ozaki 4/6 6/4 6/3
Ruth Seaborne 2/6 6/3 6/4
Indy De Vroome 7/5 7/6(5)
Aliaksandra Sasnovich 6/2 6/1
Donna Vekic 1/6 6/3 6/4
Barbora Krejcikova 6/7(2) 6/4 6/4
Nao Hibino 6/2 7/6(5)
Yulia Putintseva [7] 6/1 6/1
Eugenie Bouchard [5] 6/4 6/2
Barbara Haas 6/0 6/4
Krista Hardebeck
Alison Van Uytvanck [10] 6/3 6/0
Jesika Maleckova [15] 6/4 6/2
Daneika Borthwick 6/2 6/2
Catherine Harrison 6/2 7/6(7)
Irina Khromacheva [3] 6/3 6/2
Montserrat Gonzalez [6] 6/4 6/2
Sofiya Kovalets 7/5 6/4
Francesca Stephenson 6/4 6/2
Petra Rohanova 7/6(6) 6/3
Anett Kontaveit [13] 6/2 5/7 6/4
Lucia Butkovska
Stephanie Nauta 7/6(3) 7/6(6)
Caroline Garcia [2] 6/2 6/4

Third Round:
Kateryna Kozlova
Ellen Allgurin 2/6 7/5 6/2
Victoria Duval [16]
Victoria Duval [16] 6/1 6/2
Ashleigh Barty [12]
Ashleigh Barty [12] 6/1 6/2
Madison Keys
Madison Keys 6/2 6/1
Risa Ozaki
Risa Ozaki 6/2 3/6 6/4
Indy De Vroome
Indy De Vroome 6/2 6/3
Donna Vekic
Donna Vekic 6/2 6/4
Yulia Putintseva [7]
Yulia Putintseva [7] 6/2 6/4
Eugenie Bouchard [5]
Eugenie Bouchard [5] 6/0 6/4
Krista Hardebeck
Krista Hardebeck 3/6 6/3 6/4
Daneika Borthwick
Irina Khromacheva [3]
Irina Khromacheva [3] 6/4 6/7(6) 6/2
Montserrat Gonzalez [6]
Montserrat Gonzalez [6] 6/0 6/2
Petra Rohanova
Petra Rohanova 6/2 7/5
Anett Kontaveit [13]
Caroline Garcia [2]
Caroline Garcia [2] 6/2 6/3

Quarter-Finals:
Victoria Duval [16]
Victoria Duval [16] 6/3 6/2
Ashleigh Barty [12]
Ashleigh Barty [12] 6/3 6/7(5) 6/4
Indy De Vroome
Indy De Vroome 6/0 6/1
Yulia Putintseva [7]
Yulia Putintseva [7] 2/6 6/2 6/3
Eugenie Bouchard [5]
Eugenie Bouchard [5] 6/3 6/4
Irina Khromacheva [3]
Irina Khromacheva [3] 6/3 6/2
Montserrat Gonzalez [6]
Montserrat Gonzalez [6] 6/3 6/3
Caroline Garcia [2]
Caroline Garcia [2] 6/2 6/7(5) 6/4

Semi-Finals:
Ashleigh Barty [12]
Ashleigh Barty [12] 6/3 6/2
Indy De Vroome 6/3 6/1
Irina Khromacheva [3]
Irina Khromacheva [3] 6/2 6/2
Caroline Garcia [2] 6/1 6/7(2) 8/6

Final:
Ashleigh Barty [12] 6/4 6/1
Irina Khromacheva [3] 7/6(5) 3/6 6/1

Winner: Ashleigh Barty [12] 7/5 7/6(3)

Heavy type denotes seeded players. The figure in brackets against names denotes the order in which they were seeded.
(WC)=Wild card. (Q)=Qualifier. (LL)=Lucky Loser.

EVENT XIV – THE GIRLS' DOUBLES CHAMPIONSHIP 2011
HOLDERS: TIMEA BABOS & SLOANE STEPHENS

The Winners became the holders, for the year only, of a Cup presented by The All England Lawn Tennis and Croquet Club.
The Winners received miniature Cups and the Runners-up received mementoes. The matches were best of three sets.

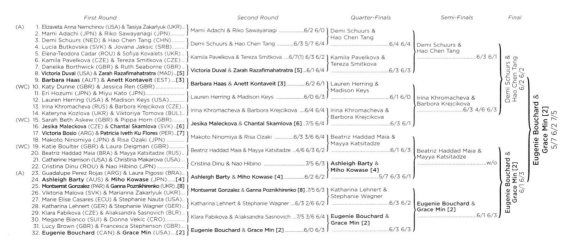

First Round:
(A) 1. Elizaveta Anna Nemchinov (USA) & Taisiya Zakarlyuk (UKR)
2. Mami Adachi (JPN) & Riko Sawayanagi (JPN)
3. Demi Schuurs (NED) & Hao Chen Tang (CHN)
4. Lucia Butkovska (SVK) & Jovana Jaksic (SRB)
5. Elena-Teodora Cadar (ROU) & Sofiya Kovalets (UKR)
6. Kamila Pavelkova (CZE) & Tereza Smitkova (CZE)
7. Daneika Borthwick (GBR) & Ruth Seaborne (GBR)
8. Victoria Duval (USA) & Zarah Razafimahatratra (MAD) [5]
9. Barbara Haas (AUT) & Anett Kontaveit (EST) [3]
(WC) 10. Katy Dunne (GBR) & Jessica Ren (GBR)
11. Eri Hozumi (JPN) & Miyu Kato (JPN)
12. Lauren Herring (USA) & Madison Keys (USA)
13. Irina Khromacheva (RUS) & Barbora Krejcikova (CZE)
14. Kateryna Kozlova (UKR) & Viktoriya Tomova (BUL)
(WC) 15. Sarah Beth Askew (GBR) & Pippa Horn (GBR)
16. Jesika Maleckova (CZE) & Chantal Skamlova (SVK) [6]
17. Victoria Bosio (ARG) & Patricia Iveth Ku Flores (PER) [7]
18. Makoto Ninomiya (JPN) & Risa Ozaki (JPN)
(WC) 19. Katie Boulter (GBR) & Laura Deigman (GBR)
20. Beatriz Haddad Maia (BRA) & Mayya Katsitadze (RUS)
21. Catherine Harrison (USA) & Christina Makarova (USA)
22. Cristina Dinu (ROU) & Nao Hibino (JPN)
(A) 23. Guadalupe Perez Rojas (ARG) & Laura Pigossi (BRA)
24. Ashleigh Barty (AUS) & Miho Kowase (JPN) [4]
25. Montserrat Gonzalez (PAR) & Ganna Poznikhirenko (UKR) [8]
26. Viktoria Malova (SVK) & Marianna Zakarlyuk (UKR)
27. Marie Elise Casares (ECU) & Stephanie Nauta (USA)
28. Katharina Lehnert (GER) & Stephanie Wagner (GER)
29. Klara Fabikova (CZE) & Aliaksandra Sasnovich (BLR)
30. Megane Bianco (SUI) & Donna Vekic (CRO)
31. Lucy Brown (GBR) & Francesca Stephenson (GBR)
32. Eugenie Bouchard (CAN) & Grace Min (USA) [2]

Second Round:
Mami Adachi & Riko Sawayanagi 6/2 6/0
Demi Schuurs & Hao Chen Tang 6/3 5/7 6/4
Kamila Pavelkova & Tereza Smitkova 6/7(1) 6/3 6/2
Victoria Duval & Zarah Razafimahatratra [5] 6/1 6/4
Barbara Haas & Anett Kontaveit [3] 6/2 6/1
Lauren Herring & Madison Keys 6/0 6/3
Irina Khromacheva & Barbora Krejcikova 6/4 6/4
Jesika Maleckova & Chantal Skamlova [6] 7/5 6/4
Makoto Ninomiya & Risa Ozaki 6/3 3/6 6/4
Beatriz Haddad Maia & Mayya Katsitadze 4/6 6/3 6/2
Cristina Dinu & Nao Hibino 7/5 6/3
Ashleigh Barty & Miho Kowase [4] 6/2 6/2
Montserrat Gonzalez & Ganna Poznikhirenko [8] 7/5 6/4
Katharina Lehnert & Stephanie Wagner 6/3 2/6 6/2
Klara Fabikova & Aliaksandra Sasnovich 7/5 3/6 6/4
Eugenie Bouchard & Grace Min [2] 6/0 6/3

Quarter-Finals:
Demi Schuurs & Hao Chen Tang 6/4 6/4
Kamila Pavelkova & Tereza Smitkova 6/3 6/2
Lauren Herring & Madison Keys 6/1 6/0
Irina Khromacheva & Barbora Krejcikova 6/3 6/1
Beatriz Haddad Maia & Mayya Katsitadze 6/1 6/3
Ashleigh Barty & Miho Kowase [4] 5/7 6/3 6/1
Katharina Lehnert & Stephanie Wagner 6/3 6/2
Eugenie Bouchard & Grace Min [2] 6/3 6/3

Semi-Finals:
Demi Schuurs & Hao Chen Tang 6/3 6/1
Irina Khromacheva & Barbora Krejcikova 6/3 4/6 6/2
Beatriz Haddad Maia & Mayya Katsitadze w/o
Eugenie Bouchard & Grace Min [2] 6/1 6/3

Final:
Demi Schuurs & Hao Chen Tang 6/2 6/2
Eugenie Bouchard & Grace Min [2] 5/7 6/2 7/5

Winner: Eugenie Bouchard & Grace Min [2] 5/7 6/2 7/5

Heavy type denotes seeded players. The figure in brackets against names denotes the order in which they were seeded.
(A)=Alternates. (WC)=Wild card.

Year	Champion / Runner-up		Year	Champion / Runner-up		Year	Champion / Runner-up		Year	Champion / Runner-up		Year	Champion / Runner-up
1877	S. W. Gore / W. C. Marshall		1906	H. L. Doherty / F. L. Riseley	*	1939	R. L. Riggs / E. T. Cooke		1974	J. S. Connors / K. R. Rosewall		2003	R. Federer / M. Philippoussis
1878	P. F. Hadow / S. W. Gore	*	1907	N. E. Brookes / A. W. Gore	*	1946	Y. Petra / G. E. Brown		1975	A. R. Ashe / J. S. Connors		2004	R. Federer / A. Roddick
* 1879	J. T. Hartley / V. St. L. Goold	*	1908	A. W. Gore / H. Roper Barrett		1947	J. Kramer / T. Brown		1976	B. Borg / I. Nastase		2005	R. Federer / A. Roddick
1880	J. T. Hartley / H. F. Lawford		1909	A. W. Gore / M. J. G. Ritchie	*	1948	R. Falkenburg / J. E. Bromwich		1977	B. Borg / J. S. Connors		2006	R. Federer / R. Nadal
1881	W. Renshaw / J. T. Hartley		1910	A. F. Wilding / A. W. Gore		1949	F. R. Schroeder / J. Drobny		1978	B. Borg / J. S.Connors		2007	R. Federer / R. Nadal
1882	W. Renshaw / E. Renshaw		1911	A. F. Wilding / H. Roper Barrett	*	1950	B. Patty / F. A. Sedgman		1979	B. Borg / R. Tanner		2008	R. Nadal / R. Federer
1883	W. Renshaw / E. Renshaw		1912	A. F. Wilding / A. W. Gore		1951	R. Savitt / K. McGregor		1980	B. Borg / J. P. McEnroe	*	2009	R. Federer / A. Roddick
1884	W. Renshaw / H. F. Lawford		1913	A. F. Wilding / M. E. McLoughlin		1952	F. A. Sedgman / J. Drobny		1981	J. P. McEnroe / B. Borg		2010	R. Nadal / T. Berdych
1885	W. Renshaw / H. F. Lawford		1914	N. E. Brookes / A. F. Wilding	*	1953	V. Seixas / K. Nielsen		1982	J. S. Connors / J. P. McEnroe		2011	N. Djokovic / R. Nadal
1886	W. Renshaw / H. F. Lawford		1919	G. L. Patterson / N. E. Brookes		1954	J. Drobny / K. R. Rosewall		1983	J. P. McEnroe / C. J. Lewis			
* 1887	H. F. Lawford / E. Renshaw		1920	W. T. Tilden / G. L. Patterson		1955	T. Trabert / K. Nielsen*		1984	J. P. McEnroe / J. S. Connors			
1888	E. Renshaw / H. F. Lawford		1921	W. T. Tilden / B. I. C. Norton		1956	L. A. Hoad / K. R. Rosewall		1985	B. Becker / K. Curren			
1889	W. Renshaw / E. Renshaw	*†	1922	G. L. Patterson / R. Lycett		1957	L. A. Hoad / A. J. Cooper		1986	B.Becker / I. Lendl			
1890	W. J. Hamilton / W. Renshaw	*	1923	W. M. Johnston / F. T. Hunter	*	1958	A. J. Cooper / N. A. Fraser		1987	P. Cash / I. Lendl			
* 1891	W. Baddeley / J. Pim	*	1924	J. Borotra / R. Lacoste	*	1959	A. Olmedo / R. Laver		1988	S. Edberg / B. Becker			
1892	W. Baddeley / J. Pim		1925	R. Lacoste / J. Borotra	*	1960	N. A. Fraser / R. Laver		1989	B. Becker / S. Edberg			
1893	J. Pim / W. Baddeley	*	1926	J. Borotra / H. Kinsey		1961	R. Laver / C. R. McKinley		1990	S. Edberg / B. Becker			
1894	J. Pim / W. Baddeley		1927	H. Cochet / J. Borotra		1962	R. Laver / M. F. Mulligan		1991	M. Stich / B. Becker			
* 1895	W. Baddeley / W. V. Eaves		1928	R. Lacoste / H. Cochet	*	1963	C. R. McKinley / F. S. Stolle		1992	A. Agassi / G. Ivanisevic			
1896	H. S. Mahony / W. Baddeley	*	1929	H. Cochet / J. Borotra		1964	R. Emerson / F. S. Stolle		1993	P. Sampras / J. Courier			
1897	R. F. Doherty / H. S. Mahony		1930	W. T. Tilden / W. Allison		1965	R. Emerson / F. S. Stolle		1994	P. Sampras / G. Ivanisevic			
1898	R. F. Doherty / H. L . Doherty	*	1931	S. B. Wood / F. X. Shields		1966	M. Santana / R. D. Ralston		1995	P. Sampras / B. Becker			
1899	R. F. Doherty / A. W. Gore		1932	H. E. Vines / H. W. Austin		1967	J. D. Newcombe / W. P. Bungert		1996	R. Krajicek / M. Washington			
1900	R. F. Doherty / S. H. Smith		1933	J. H. Crawford / H. E. Vines		1968	R. Laver / A. D. Roche		1997	P. Sampras / C. Pioline			
1901	A. W. Gore / R. F. Doherty		1934	F. J. Perry / J. H. Crawford		1969	R. Laver / J. D. Newcombe		1998	P. Sampras / G. Ivanisevic			
1902	H. L. Doherty / A. W. Gore		1935	F. J. Perry / G. von Cramm		1970	J. D. Newcombe / K. R. Rosewall		1999	P. Sampras / A. Agassi			
1903	H. L. Doherty / F. L. Riseley		1936	F. J. Perry / G. von Cramm		1971	J. D. Newcombe / S. R. Smith		2000	P. Sampras / P. Rafter			
1904	H. L. Doherty / F. L. Riseley	*	1937	J. D. Budge / G. von Cramm	*	1972	S. R. Smith / I. Nastase		2001	G. Ivanisevic / P. Rafter			
1905	H. L. Doherty / N. E. Brookes		1938	J. D. Budge / H. W. Austin	*	1973	J. Kodes / A. Metreveli		2002	L. Hewitt / D. Nalbandian			

For the years 1913, 1914 and 1919-1923 inclusive the above records include the "World's Championships on Grass" granted to The Lawn Tennis Association by The International Lawn Tennis Federation. This title was then abolished and commencing in 1924 they became The Official Lawn Tennis Championships recognised by The International Lawn Tennis Federation. Prior to 1922 the holders in the Singles Events and Gentlemen's Doubles did not compete in the Championships but met the winners of these events in the Challenge Rounds.

† Challenge Round abolished: holders subsequently played through. * The holder did not defend the title.

THE CHAMPIONSHIP ROLL
LADIES' SINGLES—CHAMPIONS & RUNNERS UP

1884 Miss M. Watson	*Miss L. Watson*
1885 Miss M. Watson	*Miss B. Bingley*
1886 Miss B. Bingley	*Miss M. Watson*
1887 Miss L. Dod	*Miss B. Bingley*
1888 Miss L. Dod	*Mrs. G. W. Hillyard*
* 1889 Mrs. G. W. Hillyard	*Miss L. Rice*
* 1890 Miss L. Rice	*Miss M. Jacks*
* 1891 Miss L. Dod	*Mrs. G. W. Hillyard*
1892 Miss L. Dod	*Mrs. G. W. Hillyard*
1893 Miss L. Dod	*Mrs. G. W. Hillyard*
* 1894 Mrs. G. W. Hillyard	*Miss E. L. Austin*
* 1895 Miss C. Cooper	*Miss H. Jackson*
1896 Miss C. Cooper	*Mrs. W. H.Pickering*
1897 Mrs. G. W. Hillyard	*Miss C. Cooper*
* 1898 Miss C. Cooper	*Miss L Martin*
1899 Mrs. G. W. Hillyard	*Miss C. Cooper*
1900 Mrs. G. W. Hillyard	*Miss C. Cooper*
1901 Mrs. A. Sterry	*Mrs. G. W. Hillyard*
1902 Miss M. E. Robb	*Mrs. A. Sterry*
* 1903 Miss D. K. Douglass	*Miss E. W. Thomson*
1904 Miss D. K. Douglass	*Mrs. A. Sterry*
1905 Miss M. Sutton	*Miss D. K. Douglass*
1906 Miss D. K. Douglass	*Miss M. Sutton*
1907 Miss M. Sutton	*Mrs. Lambert Chambers*
* 1908 Mrs. A. Sterry	*Miss A. M. Morton*
* 1909 Miss D. P. Boothby	*Miss A. M. Morton*
1910 Mrs. Lambert Chambers	*Miss D. P. Boothby*
1911 Mrs. Lambert Chambers	*Miss D. P. Boothby*

* 1912 Mrs. D. R. Larcombe	*Mrs. A. Sterry*
* 1913 Mrs. Lambert Chambers	*Mrs. R. J. McNair*
1914 Mrs. Lambert Chambers	*Mrs. D. R. Larcombe*
1919 Miss S. Lenglen	*Mrs. Lambert Chambers*
1920 Miss S. Lenglen	*Mrs. Lambert Chambers*
1921 Miss S. Lenglen	*Miss E. Ryan*
† 1922 Miss S. Lenglen	*Mrs. F. Mallory*
1923 Miss S. Lenglen	*Miss K. McKane*
1924 Miss K. McKane	*Miss H. Wills*
1925 Miss S. Lenglen	*Miss J. Fry*
1926 Mrs. L. A. Godfree	*Miss L. de Alvarez*
1927 Miss H. Wills	*Miss L. de Alvarez*
1928 Miss H. Wills	*Miss L. de Alvarez*
1929 Miss H. Wills	*Miss H. H. Jacobs*
1930 Mrs. F. S. Moody	*Miss E. Ryan*
* 1931 Miss C. Aussem	*Miss H. Krahwinkel*
* 1932 Mrs. F. S. Moody	*Miss H. H. Jacobs*
1933 Mrs. F. S. Moody	*Miss D. E. Round*
* 1934 Miss D. E. Round	*Miss H. H. Jacobs*
1935 Mrs. F. S. Moody	*Miss H. H. Jacobs*
* 1936 Miss H. H. Jacobs	*Miss S. Sperling*
1937 Mrs D. E. Round	*Miss J. Jedrzejowska*
* 1938 Mrs. F. S. Moody	*Miss H. H. Jacobs*
* 1939 Miss A. Marble	*Miss K. E. Stammers*
* 1946 Miss P. Betz	*Miss L. Brough*
* 1947 Miss M. Osborne	*Miss D. Hart*
1948 Miss L. Brough	*Miss D. Hart*
1949 Miss L. Brough	*Mrs. W. du Pont*

1950 Miss L. Brough	*Mrs. W. du Pont*
1951 Miss D. Hart	*Miss S. Fry*
1952 Miss M. Connolly	*Miss L. Brough*
1953 Miss M. Connolly	*Miss D. Hart*
1954 Miss M. Connolly	*Miss L. Brough*
* 1955 Miss L. Brough	*Mrs. J. G. Fleitz*
1956 Miss S. Fry	*Miss A. Buxton*
* 1957 Miss A. Gibson	*Miss D. R. Hard*
1958 Miss A. Gibson	*Miss A. Mortimer*
* 1959 Miss M. E. Bueno	*Miss D. R. Hard*
1960 Miss M. E. Bueno	*Miss S. Reynolds*
* 1961 Miss A. Mortimer	*Miss C. C. Truman*
1962 Mrs. J. R. Susman	*Mrs. V. Sukova*
* 1963 Miss M. Smith	*Miss B. J. Moffitt*
1964 Miss M. E. Bueno	*Miss M. Smith*
1965 Miss M. Smith	*Miss M. E. Bueno*
1966 Mrs. L. W. King	*Miss M. E. Bueno*
1967 Mrs. L. W. King	*Mrs. P. F. Jones*
1968 Mrs. L. W. King	*Miss J. A. M. Tegart*
1969 Mrs. P. F. Jones	*Mrs. L. W. King*
* 1970 Mrs. B. M. Court	*Mrs. L. W. King*
1971 Miss E. F. Goolagong	*Mrs. B. M. Court*
1972 Mrs. L. W. King	*Miss E. F. Goolagong*
1973 Mrs. L. W. King	*Miss C. M. Evert*
1974 Miss C. M. Evert	*Mrs. O. Morozova*
1975 Mrs. L. W. King	*Mrs. R. Cawley*
* 1976 Miss C. M. Evert	*Mrs. R. Cawley*
1977 Miss S. V. Wade	*Miss B. F. Stove*

1978 Miss M. Navratilova	*Miss C. M. Evert*
1979 Miss M. Navratilova	*Mrs. J. M. Lloyd*
1980 Mrs. R. Cawley	*Mrs. J. M. Lloyd*
* 1981 Mrs. J. M. Lloyd	*Miss H. Mandlikova*
1982 Miss M. Navratilova	*Mrs. J. M. Lloyd*
1983 Miss M. Navratilova	*Miss A. Jaeger*
1984 Miss M. Navratilova	*Mrs. J. M. Lloyd*
1985 Miss M. Navratilova	*Mrs. J. M. Lloyd*
1986 Miss M. Navratilova	*Miss H. Mandlikova*
1987 Miss M. Navratilova	*Miss S. Graf*
1988 Miss S. Graf	*Miss M. Navratilova*
1989 Miss S. Graf	*Miss M. Navratilova*
1990 Miss M. Navratilova	*Miss Z. Garrison*
1991 Miss S. Graf	*Miss G. Sabatini*
1992 Miss S. Graf	*Miss M. Seles*
1993 Miss S. Graf	*Miss J. Novotna*
1994 Miss C. Martinez	*Miss M. Navratilova*
1995 Miss S. Graf	*Miss A. Sanchez Vicario*
1996 Miss S. Graf	*Miss A. Sanchez Vicario*
* 1997 Miss M. Hingis	*Miss J. Novotna*
1998 Miss J. Novotna	*Miss N. Tauziat*
1999 Miss L.A. Davenport	*Miss S. Graf*
2000 Miss V. Williams	*Miss L.A. Davenport*
2001 Miss V. Williams	*Miss J. Henin*
2002 Miss S. Williams	*Miss V. Williams*
2003 Miss S. Williams	*Miss V. Williams*
2004 Miss M. Sharapova	*Miss S. Williams*
2005 Miss V. Williams	*Miss L. Davenport*

2006 Miss A. Mauresmo	*Mrs J. Henin-Hardenne*
2007 Miss V. Williams	*Miss M. Bartoli*
2008 Miss V. Williams	*Miss S. Williams*
2009 Miss S. Williams	*Miss V. Williams*
2010 Miss S. Williams	*Miss V. Zvonareva*
2011 Miss P. Kvitova	*Miss M. Sharapova*

MAIDEN NAMES OF LADY CHAMPIONS (*In the tables the following have been recorded in both married and single identities*)

Mrs. R. Cawley ....Miss E. F. Goolagong	Mrs J. Henin-Hardenne..............Miss J. Henin	Mrs. O. Morozova........................Miss O. Morozova
Mrs. Lambert Chambers..........Miss D. K. Douglass	Mrs. G. W. Hillyard....................Miss B. Bingley	Mrs. L. E. G. Price ....Miss S. Reynolds
Mrs. B. M. Court......................Miss M. Smith	Mrs. P. F. Jones ....Miss A. S. Haydon	Mrs. G. E. Reid.........................Miss K. Melville
Mrs. B. C. Covell....................Miss P. L. Howkins	Mrs. L. W. King ....Miss B. J. Moffitt	Mrs. P. D. Smylie.......................Miss E. M. Sayers
Mrs. D. E. Dalton......................Miss J. A. M. Tegart	Mrs. M. R. King..........................Miss P. E. Mudford	Frau. S. Sperling...............................Fraulein H. Krahwinkel
Mrs. W. du Pont ....Miss M. Osborne	Mrs. D. R. Larcombe ....Miss E. W. Thomson	Mrs. A. Sterry ....Miss C. Cooper
Mrs. L. A. Godfree...................Miss K. McKane	Mrs. J. M. Lloyd ....Miss C. M. Evert	Mrs. J. R. Susman ....Miss K. Hantze
Mrs. H. F. Gourlay Cawley........Miss H. F. Gourlay	Mrs. F. S. Moody ....Miss H. Wills	

THE CHAMPIONSHIP ROLL

GENTLEMEN'S DOUBLES—CHAMPIONS & RUNNERS UP

1879 L. R. Erskine & H. F. Lawford
F. Durant & G. E. Tabor
1880 W. Renshaw & E. Renshaw
O. E. Woodhouse & C. J. Cole
1881 W. Renshaw & E. Renshaw
W. J. Down & H. Vaughan
1882 J. T. Hartley & R. T. Richardson
J. G. Horn & C. B. Russell
1883 C. W. Grinstead & C. E. Welldon
C. B. Russell & R. T. Milford
1884 W. Renshaw & E. Renshaw
E. W. Lewis & E. L Williams
1885 W. Renshaw & E. Renshaw
C. E. Farrer & A. J. Stanley
1886 W. Renshaw & E. Renshaw
C. E. Farrer & A. J. Stanley
1887 P. Bowes-Lyon & H. W. W. Wilberforce
J. H. Crispe & E. Barratt Smith
1888 W. Renshaw & E. Renshaw
P Bowes-Lyon & H. W. W. Wilberforce
1889 W. Renshaw & E. Renshaw
E. W. Lewis & G. W. Hillyard
1890 J. Pim & F. O. Stoker
E. W. Lewis & G. W. Hillyard
1891 W. Baddeley & H. Baddeley
J. Pim & F. O. Stoker
1892 H. S. Barlow & E. W. Lewis
W. Baddeley & H. Baddeley
1893 J. Pim & F. O. Stoker
E. W. Lewis & H. S. Barlow
1894 W. Baddeley & H. Baddeley
H. S. Barlow & C. H. Martin
1895 W. Baddeley & H. Baddeley
E. W. Lewis & W. V. Eaves
1896 W. Baddeley & H. Baddeley
R. F. Doherty & H. A. Nisbet
1897 R. F. Doherty & H. L. Doherty
W. Baddeley & H. Baddeley
1898 R. F. Doherty & H. L . Doherty
H. A. Nisbet & C. Hobart
1899 R. F. Doherty & H. L. Doherty
H. A. Nisbet & C. Hobart
1900 R. F. Doherty & H. L. Doherty
H. Roper Barrett & H. A. Nisbet
1901 R. F. Doherty & H. L. Doherty
Dwight Davis & Holcombe Ward
1902 S. H. Smith & F. L. Riseley
R. F. Doherty & H. L. Doherty
1903 R. F. Doherty & H. L. Doherty
S. H. Smith & F. L. Riseley
1904 R. F. Doherty & H. L. Doherty
S. H. Smith & F. L. Riseley
1905 R. F. Doherty & H. L. Doherty
S. H. Smith & F. L. Riseley
1906 S. H. Smith & F. L. Riseley
R. F. Doherty & H. L. Doherty
1907 N. E. Brookes & A. F. Wilding
B. C. Wright & K. H. Behr
1908 A. F. Wilding & M. J. G. Ritchie
A. W. Gore & H. Roper Barrett
1909 A. W. Gore & H. Roper Barrett
S. N. Doust & H. A. Parker
1910 A. F. Wilding & M. J. G. Ritchie
A. W. Gore & H. Roper Barrett
1911 M. Decugis & A. H. Gobert
M. J. G. Ritchie & A. F. Wilding
1912 H. Roper Barrett & C. P. Dixon
M. Decugis & A. H. Gobert
1913 H. Roper Barrett & C. P. Dixon
F. W. Rahe & H. Kleinschroth
1914 N. E. Brookes & A. F. Wilding
H. Roper Barrett & C. P. Dixon
1919 R. V. Thomas & P. O'Hara-Wood
R. Lycett & R. W. Heath
1920 R. N. Williams & C. S. Garland
A. R. F. Kingscote & J. C. Parke
1921 R. Lycett & M. Woosnam
F. G. Lowe & A. H. Lowe
1922 R. Lycett & J. O. Anderson
G. L. Patterson & P. O'Hara-Wood
1923 R. Lycett & L. A. Godfree
Count de Gomar & E. Flaquer
1924 F. T. Hunter & V. Richards
R. N. Williams & W. M. Washburn
1925 J. Borotra & R. Lacoste
J. Hennessey & R. Casey
1926 H. Cochet & J. Brugnon
V. Richards & H. Kinsey
1927 F. T. Hunter & W. T. Tilden
J. Brugnon & H. Cochet
1928 H. Cochet & J. Brugnon
G. L. Patterson & J. B. Hawkes
1929 W. Allison & J. Van Ryn
J. C. Gregory & I. G. Collins
1930 W. Allison & J. Van Ryn
J. H. Doeg & G. M. Lott
1931 G. M Lott & J. Van Ryn
H. Cochet & J. Brugnon
1932 J. Borotra & J. Brugnon
G. P. Hughes & F. J. Perry
1933 J. Borotra & J. Brugnon
R. Nunoi & J. Satoh
1934 G. M. Lott & L. R. Stoefen
J. Borotra & J. Brugnon
1935 J. H. Crawford & A. K. Quist
W. Allison & J. Van Ryn
1936 G. P. Hughes & C. R. D. Tuckey
C. E. Hare & F. H. D. Wilde
1937 J. D. Budge & G. Mako
G. P. Hughes & C. R. D. Tuckey
1938 J. D. Budge & G. Mako
H. Henkel & G. von Metaxa
1939 R. L. Riggs & E. T. Cooke
C. E. Hare & F. H. D. Wilde
1946 T. Brown & J. Kramer
G. E. Brown & D. Pails
1947 R. Falkenburg & J. Kramer
A. J. Mottram & O. W. Sidwell
1948 J. E. Bromwich & F. A. Sedgman
T. Brown & G. Mulloy
1949 R. Gonzales & F. Parker
G. Mulloy & F. R. Schroeder
1950 J. E. Bromwich & A. K. Quist
G. E. Brown & O. W Sidwell
1951 K. McGregor & F. A. Sedgman
J. Drobny & E. W. Sturgess
1952 K. McGregor & F. A. Sedgman
V. Seixas & E. W. Sturgess
1953 L. A. Hoad & K. R. Rosewall
R. N. Hartwig & M. G. Rose
1954 R. N. Hartwig & M. G. Rose
V. Seixas & T. Trabert
1955 R. N. Hartwig & L. A. Hoad
N. A. Fraser & K. R. Rosewall
1956 L. A. Hoad & K. R. Rosewall
N. Pietrangeli & O. Sirola
1957 G. Mulloy & B. Patty
N. A. Fraser & L. A. Hoad
1958 S. Davidson & U. Schmidt
A. J. Cooper & N. A. Fraser
1959 R. Emerson & N. A. Fraser
R. Laver & R. Mark
1960 R. H. Osuna & R. D. Ralston
M. G. Davies & R. K. Wilson
1961 R. Emerson & N. A. Fraser
R. A. J. Hewitt & F. S. Stolle
1962 R. A. J. Hewitt & F. S. Stolle
B. Jovanovic & N. Pilic
1963 R. H. Osuna & A. Palafox
J. C. Barclay & P. Darmon
1964 R. A. J. Hewitt & F. S. Stolle
R. Emerson & K. N. Fletcher
1965 J. D. Newcombe & A. D. Roche
K. N. Fletcher & R. A. J. Hewitt
1966 K. N. Fletcher & J. D. Newcombe
W. W. Bowrey & O. K. Davidson
1967 R. A. J. Hewitt & F. D. McMillan
R. Emerson & K. N. Fletcher
1968 J. D. Newcombe & A. D. Roche
K. R. Rosewall & F. S. Stolle
1969 J. D. Newcombe & A. D. Roche
T. S. Okker & M. C. Reissen
1970 J. D. Newcombe & A. D. Roche
K. R. Rosewall & F. S. Stolle
1971 R. S. Emerson & R. G. Laver
A. R. Ashe & R. D. Ralston
1972 R. A. J. Hewitt & F. D. McMillan
S. R. Smith & E. J. van Dillen
1973 J. S. Connors & I. Nastase
J. R. Cooper & N. A. Fraser
1974 J. D. Newcombe & A. D. Roche
R. C. Lutz & S. R. Smith
1975 V. Gerulaitis & A. Mayer
C. Dowdeswell & A. J. Stone
1976 B. E. Gottfried & R. Ramirez
R. L. Case & G. Masters
1977 R. L. Case & G. Masters
J. G. Alexander & P. C. Dent
1978 R. A. J. Hewitt & F. D. McMillan
P. Fleming & J. P. McEnroe
1979 P. Fleming & J. P . McEnroe
B. E. Gottfried & R. Ramirez
1980 P. McNamara & P. McNamee
R. C. Lutz & S. R. Smith
1981 P. Fleming & J. P. McEnroe
R. C. Lutz & S. R. Smith
1982 P. McNamara & P. McNamee
P. Fleming & J. P. McEnroe
1983 P. Fleming & J. P McEnroe
T. E. Gullikson & T. R. Gullikson
1984 P. Fleming & J. P. McEnroe
P. Cash & P. McNamee
1985 H. P. Guenthardt & B. Taroczy
P. Cash & J. B. Fitzgerald
1986 J. Nystrom & M. Wilander
G. Donnelly & P. Fleming
1987 K. Flach & R. Seguso
S. Casal & E. Sanchez
1988 K. Flach & R. Seguso
J. B. Fitzgerald & A. Jarryd
1989 J. B. Fitzgerald & A. Jarryd
R. Leach & J. Pugh
1990 R. Leach & J. Pugh
P. Aldrich & D. T. Visser
1991 J. B. Fitzgerald & A. Jarryd
J. Frana & L. Lavalle
1992 J. P. McEnroe & M. Stich
J. Grabb & R. A. Reneberg
1993 T. A. Woodbridge & M. Woodforde
G. Connell & P. Galbraith
1994 T. A. Woodbridge & M. Woodforde
G. Connell & P. Galbraith
1995 T. A. Woodbridge & M. Woodforde
R. Leach & S. Melville
1996 T. A. Woodbridge & M. Woodforde
B. Black & G. Connell
1997 T. A. Woodbridge & M. Woodforde
J. Eltingh & P. Haarhuis
1998 J. Eltingh & P. Haarhuis
T. A. Woodbridge & M. Woodforde
1999 M. Bhupathi & L. Paes
P. Haarhuis & J. Palmer
2000 T. A. Woodbridge & M. Woodforde
P. Haarhuis & S. Stolle
2001 D. Johnson & J. Palmer
J. Novak & D. Rikl
2002 J. Bjorkman & T. A Woodbridge
M. Knowles & D. Nestor
2003 J. Bjorkman & T. A Woodbridge
M. Bhupathi & M. Mirnyi
2004 J. Bjorkman & T. A Woodbridge
J. Knowle & N. Zimonjic
2005 S. Huss & W. Moodie
B. Bryan & M. Bryan
2006 B. Bryan & M. Bryan
F. Santoro & N. Zimonjic
2007 A. Clement & M. Llodra
B. Bryan & M. Bryan
2008 D. Nestor & N. Zimonjic
J. Bjorkman & K. Ullyett
2009 D. Nestor & N. Zimonjic
B. Bryan & M. Bryan
2010 J. Melzer & P. Petzschner
R. Lindstedt & H. Tecau
2011 B. Bryan & M. Bryan
R. Linstedt & H. Tecau

LADIES' DOUBLES—CHAMPIONS & RUNNERS UP

1913 Mrs. R. J. McNair & Miss D. P. Boothby
Mrs. A. Sterry & Mrs. Lambert Chambers
1914 Miss E. Ryan & Miss A. M. Morton
Mrs. D. R. Larcombe & Mrs. F. J. Hannam
1919 Miss S. Lenglen & Miss E. Ryan
Mrs. Lambert Chambers & Mrs. D. R. Larcombe
1920 Miss S. Lenglen & Miss E. Ryan
Mrs. Lambert Chambers & Mrs. D. R. Larcombe
1921 Miss S. Lenglen & Miss E. Ryan
Mrs. A. E. Beamish & Mrs. G. E. Peacock
1922 Miss S. Lenglen & Miss E. Ryan
Mrs. A. D. Stocks & Miss K. McKane
1923 Miss S. Lenglen & Miss E. Ryan
Miss J. Austin & Miss E. L. Colyer
1924 Mrs. H. Wightman & Miss H. Wills
Mrs. B. C. Covell & Miss K. McKane
1925 Miss S. Lenglen & Miss E. Ryan
Mrs. A. V. Bridge & Mrs. C. G. McIlquham
1926 Miss E. Ryan & Miss M. K. Browne
Mrs. L. A. Godfree & Miss E. L. Colyer
1927 Miss H. Wills & Miss E. Ryan
Miss E. L. Heine & Mrs. G. E. Peacock
1928 Mrs. Holcroft-Watson & Miss P. Saunders
Miss E. H. Harvey & Miss E. Bennett
1929 Mrs. Holcroft-Watson & Mrs. L.R.C. Michell
Mrs. B. C. Covell & Mrs. D. C. Shepherd-Barron
1930 Mrs. F. S. Moody & Miss E. Ryan
Miss E. Cross & Miss S. Palfrey
1931 Mrs.D.C. Shepherd-Barron & Miss P.E. Mudford
Miss D. Metaxa & Miss J. Sigart
1932 Miss D. Metaxa & Miss J. Sigart
Miss E. Ryan & Miss H. H. Jacobs
1933 Mrs. R. Mathieu & Miss E. Ryan
Miss F. James & Miss A. M. Yorke
1934 Mrs. R. Mathieu & Miss E. Ryan
Mrs. D. Andrus & Mrs. S. Henrotin
1935 Miss F. James & Miss K. E. Stammers
Mrs. R. Mathieu & Mrs S. Sperling
1936 Miss F. James & Miss K. E. Stammers
Mrs. S. P. Fabyan & Miss H. H. Jacobs
1937 Mrs. R. Mathieu & Miss A. M. Yorke
Mrs. M. R. King & Mrs. J. B. Pittman
1938 Mrs. S. P. Fabyan & Miss A. Marble
Mrs. R. Mathieu & Miss A. M. Yorke
1939 Mrs S. P. Fabyan & Miss A. Marble
Miss H. H. Jacobs & Miss A. M. Yorke
1946 Miss L. Brough & Miss M. Osborne
Miss P. Betz & Miss D. Hart
1947 Miss D. Hart & Mrs. P. C. Todd
Miss L. Brough & Miss M. Osborne
1948 Miss L. Brough & Mrs. W. du Pont
Miss D. Hart & Mrs. P. C. Todd
1949 Miss L. Brough & Mrs. W. du Pont
Miss G. Moran & Mrs. P. C. Todd
1950 Miss L. Brough & Mrs. W. du Pont
Miss S. Fry & Miss D. Hart
1951 Miss S. Fry & Miss D. Hart
Miss L. Brough & Mrs. W. du Pont
1952 Miss S. Fry & Miss D. Hart
Miss L. Brough & Miss M. Connolly
1953 Miss S. Fry & Miss D. Hart
Miss M. Connolly & Miss J. Sampson
1954 Miss L. Brough & Mrs. W. du Pont
Miss S. Fry & Miss D. Hart
1955 Miss A. Mortimer & Miss J. A. Shilcock
Miss S. J. Bloomer & Miss P. E. Ward
1956 Miss A. Buxton & Miss A. Gibson
Miss F. Muller & Miss D. G. Seeney
1957 Miss A. Gibson & Miss D. R. Hard
Mrs. K. Hawton & Mrs. T. D. Long
1958 Miss M. E. Bueno & Miss A. Gibson
Mrs. W. du Pont & Miss M. Varner
1959 Miss J. Arth & Miss D. R. Hard
Mrs. J. G. Fleitz & Miss C. C. Truman
1960 Miss M. E. Bueno & Miss D. R. Hard
Miss S. Reynolds & Miss R. Schuurman
1961 Miss K. Hantze & Miss B. J. Moffitt
Miss J. Lehane & Miss M. Smith
1962 Miss B. J. Moffitt & Mrs. J. R. Susman
Mrs. L. E. G. Price & Miss R. Schuurman
1963 Miss M. E. Bueno & Miss D. R. Hard
Miss R. A. Ebbern & Miss M. Smith
1964 Miss M. Smith & Miss L. R. Turner
Miss B. J. Moffitt & Mrs. J. R. Susman
1965 Miss M. E. Bueno & Miss B. J. Moffitt
Miss F. Durr & Miss J. LieVrig
1966 Miss M. E. Bueno & Miss N. Richey
Miss M. Smith & Miss J. A. M. Tegart
1967 Miss R. Casals & Mrs. L. W. King
Miss M. E. Bueno & Miss N. Richey
1968 Miss R. Casals & Mrs. L. W. King
Miss F. Durr & Mrs. P. F. Jones
1969 Mrs. B. M. Court & Miss J. A. M. Tegart
Miss P. S. A. Hogan & Miss M. Michel
1970 Miss R. Casals & Mrs. L. W. King
Miss F. Durr & Miss S. V. Wade
1971 Miss R. Casals & Mrs. L. W. King
Mrs. B. M. Court & Miss E. F. Goolagong
1972 Mrs. L. W. King & Miss B. F. Stove
Mrs. D. E. Dalton & Miss F. Durr
1973 Miss R. Casals & Mrs. L. W. King
Miss F. Durr & Miss B. F. Stove
1974 Miss E. F. Goolagong & Miss M. Michel
Miss H. F. Gourlay & Miss K. M. Krantzcke
1975 Miss A. Kiyomura & Miss K. Sawamatsu
Miss F. Durr & Miss B. F. Stove
1976 Miss C. M. Evert & Miss M. Navratilova
Mrs. L. W. King & Miss B. F. Stove
1977 Mrs. H. F. Gourlay Cawley & Miss J. C. Russell
Miss M. Navratilova & Miss B. F . Stove
1978 Mrs. G. E. Reid & Miss. W. M. Turnbull
Miss M. Jausovec & Miss V. Ruzici
1979 Mrs. L. W. King & Miss M. Navratilova
Miss B. F. Stove & Miss W. M. Turnbull
1980 Miss K. Jordan & Miss A. E. Smith
Miss R. Casals & Miss W. M. Turnbull
1981 Miss M. Navratilova & Miss P. H. Shriver
Miss K. Jordan & Miss A. E. Smith
1982 Miss M. Navratilova & Miss P. H. Shriver
Miss K. Jordan & Miss A. E. Smith
1983 Miss M. Navratilova & Miss P. H. Shriver
Miss R. Casals & Miss W. M. Turnbull
1984 Miss M. Navratilova & Miss P. H. Shriver
Miss K. Jordan & Miss A. E. Smith
1985 Miss K. Jordan & Mrs. P. D. Smylie
Miss M. Navratilova & Miss P. H. Shriver
1986 Miss M. Navratilova & Miss P. H. Shriver
Miss H. Mandlikova & Miss W. M. Turnbull
1987 Miss C. Kohde-Kilsch & Miss H. Sukova
Miss B. Nagelsen & Mrs. P. D. Smylie
1988 Miss S. Graf & Miss G. Sabatini
Miss L. Savchenko & Miss N. Zvereva
1989 Miss J. Novotna & Miss H. Sukova
Miss L. Savchenko & Miss N. Zvereva
1990 Miss J. Novotna & Miss H. Sukova
Miss K. Jordan & Mrs. P. D. Smylie
1991 Miss L. Savchenko & Miss N. Zvereva
Miss G. Fernandez & Miss J. Novotna
1992 Miss G. Fernandez & Miss N. Zvereva
Miss J. Novotna & Mrs. L. Savchenko-Neiland
1993 Miss G. Fernandez & Miss N. Zvereva
Mrs. L. Neiland & Miss J. Novotna
1994 Miss G. Fernandez & Miss N. Zvereva
Miss J. Novotna & Miss A. Sanchez Vicario
1995 Miss J. Novotna & Miss A. Sanchez Vicario
Miss G. Fernandez & Miss N. Zvereva
1996 Miss M. Hingis & Miss H. Sukova
Miss M.J. McGrath & Mrs. L. Neiland
1997 Miss G. Fernandez & Miss N. Zvereva
Miss N.J. Arendt & Miss M.M. Bollegraf
1998 Miss M. Hingis & Miss J. Novotna
Miss L.A. Davenport & Miss N. Zvereva
1999 Miss L.A. Davenport & Miss C. Morariu
Miss M. de Swardt & Miss E. Tatarkova
2000 Miss S. Williams & Miss V. Williams
Mrs J. Halard-Decugis & Miss A. Sugiyama
2001 Miss L.M. Raymond & Miss R.P. Stubbs
Miss K. Clijsters & Miss A. Sugiyama
2002 Miss S. Williams & Miss V. Williams
Miss V. Ruano Pascual & Miss P. Suarez
2003 Miss K. Clijsters & Miss A. Sugiyama
Miss V. Ruano Pascual & Miss P. Suarez
2004 Miss C. Black & Miss R.P. Stubbs
Mrs L. Huber & Miss A. Sugiyama
2005 Miss C. Black & Mrs L. Huber
Miss S. Kuznetsova & Miss A. Muresmo
2006 Miss Z. Yan & Miss J. Zheng
Miss V. Ruano Pascual & Miss P. Suarez
2007 Miss C. Black & Mrs L. Huber
Miss K. Srebotnik & Miss A. Sugiyama
2008 Miss S. Williams & Miss V. Williams
Miss L.M. Raymond & Miss S. Stosur
2009 Miss S. Williams & Miss V. Williams
Miss S. Stosur & Miss R.P. Stubbs
2010 Miss V. King & Miss Y. Shvedova
Miss E. Vesnina & Miss V. Zvonareva
2011 Miss K. Peschke & Miss K. Srebotnik
Miss S. Lisicki & Miss S. Stosur

THE CHAMPIONSHIP ROLL
MIXED DOUBLES—CHAMPIONS & RUNNERS UP

1913　H. Crisp & Mrs. C. O. Tuckey
J. C. Parke & Mrs. D. R. Larcombe

1914　J. C. Parke & Mrs. D.R. Larcombe
A. F. Wilding & Miss M. Broquedis

1919　R. Lycett & Miss E. Ryan
A. D. Prebble & Mrs. Lambert Chambers

1920　G. L. Patterson & Miss S. Lenglen
R. Lycett & Miss E. Ryan

1921　R. Lycett & Miss E. Ryan
M. Woosnam & Miss P. L. Howkins

1922　P. O'Hara-Wood & Miss S. Lenglen
R. Lycett & Miss E. Ryan

1923　R. Lycett & Miss E. Ryan
L. S. Deane & Mrs. D. C. Shepherd-Barron

1924　J. B. Gilbert & Miss K. McKane
L. A. Godfree & Mrs. D. C. Shepherd-Barron

1925　J. Borotra & Miss S. Lenglen
H. L. de Morpurgo & Miss E. Ryan

1926　L. A. Godfree & Mrs. L. A. Godfree
H. Kinsey & Miss M. K. Browne

1927　F. T. Hunter & Miss E. Ryan
L. A. Godfree & Mrs. L. A. Godfree

1928　P. D. B. Spence & Miss E. Ryan
J. Crawford & Miss D. Akhurst

1929　F. T. Hunter & Miss H. Wills
I. G. Collins & Miss J. Fry

1930　J. H. Crawford & Miss E. Ryan
D. Prenn & Miss H. Krahwinkel

1931　G. M. Lott & Mrs L. A. Harper
I. G. Collins & Miss J. C. Ridley

1932　E. Maier & Miss E. Ryan
H. C. Hopman & Miss J. Sigart

1933　G. von Cramm & Miss H. Krahwinkel
N. G. Farquharson & Miss M. Heeley

1934　R. Miki & Miss D. E. Round
H. W. Austin & Mrs D. C. Shepherd-Barron

1935　F. J. Perry & Miss D. E. Round
H. C. Hopman & Mrs. H. C. Hopman

1936　F. J. Perry & Miss D. E. Round
J. D. Budge & Mrs. S. P. Fabyan

1937　J. D. Budge & Miss A. Marble
Y. Petra & Mrs. R. Mathieu

1938　J. D. Budge & Miss A. Marble
H. Henkel & Mrs. S. P. Fabyan

1939　R. L. Riggs & Miss A. Marble
F. H. D. Wilde & Miss N. B. Brown

1946　T. Brown & Miss L. Brough
G. E. Brown & Miss D. Bundy

1947　J. E. Bromwich & Miss L. Brough
C. F. Long & Mrs. N. M. Bolton

1948　J. E. Bromwich & Miss L. Brough
F. A. Sedgman & Miss D. Hart

1949　E. W. Sturgess & Mrs. S. P. Summers
J. E. Bromwich & Miss L. Brough

1950　E. W. Sturgess & Miss L. Brough
G. E. Brown & Mrs. P. C. Todd

1951　F. A. Sedgman & Miss D. Hart
M. G. Rose & Mrs. N. M. Bolton

1952　F. A. Sedgman & Miss D. Hart
E. Morea & Mrs. T. D. Long

1953　V. Seixas & Miss D. Hart
E. Morea & Miss S. Fry

1954　V. Seixas & Miss D. Hart
K. R. Rosewall & Mrs. W. du Pont

1955　V. Seixas & Miss D. Hart
E. Morea & Miss L. Brough

1956　V. Seixas & Miss S. Fry
G. Mulloy & Miss A. Gibson

1957　M. G. Rose & Miss D. R. Hard
N. A. Fraser & Miss A. Gibson

1958　R. N. Howe & Miss L. Coghlan
K. Nielsen & Miss A. Gibson

1959　R. Laver & Miss D. R. Hard
N. A. Fraser & Miss M. E. Bueno

1960　R. Laver & Miss D. R. Hard
R. N. Howe & Miss M. E. Bueno

1961　F. S. Stolle & Miss L. R. Turner
R. N. Howe & Miss E. Buding

1962　N. A. Fraser & Mrs. W. du Pont
R. D. Ralston & Miss A. S. Haydon

1963　K. N. Fletcher & Miss M. Smith
R. A. J. Hewitt & Miss D. R. Hard

1964　F. S. Stolle & Miss L. R. Turner
K. N. Fletcher & Miss M. Smith

1965　K. N. Fletcher & Miss M. Smith
A. D. Roche & Miss J. A. M. Tegart

1966　K. N. Fletcher & Miss M. Smith
R. D. Ralston amd Mrs. L. W. King

1967　O. K. Davidson & Mrs. L. W. King
K. N. Fletcher & Miss M. E. Bueno

1968　K. N. Fletcher & Mrs. B. M. Court
A. Metreveli & Miss O. Morozova

1969　F. S. Stolle & Mrs. P. F. Jones
A. D. Roche & Miss J. A. M. Tegart

1970　I. Nastase & Miss R. Casals
A. Metreveli & Miss O. Morozova

1971　O. K. Davidson & Mrs. L. W. King
M. C. Riessen & Mrs. B. M. Court

1972　I. Nastase & Miss R. Casals
K.G. Warwick & Miss E. F. Goolagong

1973　O. K. Davidson & Mrs. L. W. King
R. Ramirez & Miss J. S. Newberry

1974　O. K. Davidson & Mrs. L. W. King
M. J. Farrell & Miss L. J. Charles

1975　M. C. Riessen & Mrs. B. M. Court
A. J. Stone & Miss B. F. Stove

1976　A. D. Roche & Miss F. Durr
R. L. Stockton & Miss R. Casals

1977　R. A. J. Hewitt & Miss G. R. Stevens
F. D. McMillan & Miss B. F. Stove

1978　F. D. McMillan & Miss B. F. Stove
R. O. Ruffels & Mrs. L. W. King

1979　R. A. J. Hewitt & Miss G. R. Stevens
F. D. McMillan & Miss B. F. Stove

1980　J. R. Austin & Miss T. Austin
M. R. Edmondson & Miss D. L. Fromholtz

1981　F. D. McMillan & Miss B. F. Stove
J. R. Austin & Miss T. Austin

1982　K. Curren & Miss A. E. Smith
J. M. Lloyd & Miss W. M. Turnbull

1983　J. M. Lloyd & Miss W. M. Turnbull
S. Denton & Mrs. L. W. King

1984　J. M. Lloyd & Miss W. M. Turnbull
S. Denton & Miss K. Jordan

1985　P. McNamee & Miss M. Navratilova
J. B. Fitzgerald & Mrs. P. D. Smylie

1986　K. Flach & Miss K. Jordan
H. P. Guenthardt & Miss M. Navratilova

1987　M. J. Bates & Miss J. M. Durie
D. Cahill & Miss N. Provis

1988　S. E. Stewart & Miss Z. L. Garrison
K. Jones & Mrs. S. W. Magers

1989　J. Pugh & Miss J. Novotna
M. Kratzmann & Miss J. M. Byrne

1990　R. Leach & Miss Z. L. Garrison
J. B. Fitzgerald & Mrs P. D. Smylie

1991　J. B. Fitzgerald & Mrs. P. D. Smylie
J. Pugh & Miss N. Zvereva

1992　C. Suk & Mrs L. Savchenko-Neiland
J. Eltingh & Miss M. Oremans

1993　M. Woodforde & Miss M. Navratilova
T. Nijssen & Miss M. M. Bollegraf

1994　T. A. Woodbridge & Miss H. Sukova
T. J. Middleton & Miss L. M. McNeil

1995　J. Stark & Miss M. Navratilova
C. Suk & Miss G. Fernandez

1996　C. Suk & Miss H. Sukova
M. Woodforde & Mrs. L. Neiland

1997　C. Suk & Miss H. Sukova
A. Olhovskiy & Mrs L. Neiland

1998　M. Mirnyi & Miss S. Williams
M. Bhupathi & Miss M. Lucic

1999　L. Paes & Miss L.M. Raymond
J. Bjorkman & Miss A. Kournikova

2000　D. Johnson & Miss K. Po
L. Hewitt & Miss K. Clijsters

2001　L. Friedl & Miss D. Hantuchova
M. Bryan & Mrs L. Huber

2002　M. Bhupathi & Miss E. Likhovtseva
K. Ullyett & Miss D. Hantuchova

2003　L. Paes & Miss M. Navratilova
A. Ram & Miss A. Rodionova

2004　W. Black & Miss C. Black
T.A. Woodbridge & Miss A. Molik

2005　M. Bhupathi & Miss M. Pierce
P. Hanley & Miss T. Perebiynis

2006　A. Ram & Miss V. Zvonareva
B. Bryan & Miss V. Williams

2007　J. Murray & Miss J. Jankovic
J. Bjorkman & Miss A. Molik

2008　B. Bryan & Miss S. Stosur
M. Bryan & Miss K. Srebotnik

2009　M. Knowles & Miss A-L. Groenefeld
L. Paes & Miss C. Black

2010　L. Paes & Miss C. Black
W. Moody & Miss L. Raymond

2011　J. Melzer & Miss I. Benesova
M. Bhupathi & Miss E. Vesnina

THE CHAMPIONSHIP ROLL
BOYS' SINGLES

1947	K. Nielsen (DENMARK)	
	S. V. Davidson (SWEDEN)	
1948	S. Stockenberg (SWEDEN)	
	D. Vad (HUNGARY)	
1949	S. Stockenberg (SWEDEN)	
	J. A. T. Horn (GBR)	
1950	J. A. T. Horn (GBR)	
	K. Mobarek (EGYPT)	
1951	J. Kupferburger (SA)	
	K. Mobarek (EGYPT)	
1952	R. K. Wilson (GBR)	
	T. T. Fancutt (SA)	
1953	W. A. Knight (GBR)	
	R. Krishnan (INDIA)	
1954	R. Krishnan (INDIA)	
	A. J. Cooper (AUSTRALIA)	
1955	M. P. Hann (GBR)	
	J. E. Lundquist (SWEDEN)	
1956	R. Holmberg (USA)	
	R. G. Laver (AUSTRALIA)	
1957	J. I. Tattersall (GBR)	
	I. Ribeiro (BRAZIL)	
1958	E. Buchholz (USA)	
	P. J. Lall (INDIA)	
1959	T. Lejus (USSR)	
	R. W. Barnes (BRAZIL)	
1960	A. R. Mandelstam (SA)	
	J. Mukerjea (INDIA)	
1961	C. E. Graebner (USA)	
	E. Blanke (AUSTRIA)	
1962	S. Matthews (GBR)	
	A. Metreveli (USSR)	
1963	N. Kalogeropoulos (GREECE)	
	I. El Shafei (UAR)	

1964	I. El Shafei (UAR)	
	V. Korotkov (USSR)	
1965	V. Korotkov (USSR)	
	G. Goven (FRANCE)	
1966	V. Korotkov (USSR)	
	B. E. Fairlie (NZ)	
1967	M. Orantes (SPAIN)	
	M. S. Estep (USA)	
1968	J. G. Alexander (AUSTRALIA)	
	J. Thamin (FRANCE)	
1969	B. Bertram (SA)	
	J. G. Alexander (AUSTRALIA)	
1970	B. Bertram (SA)	
	F. Gebert (GERMANY)	
1971	R. Kreiss (USA)	
	S. A. Warboys (GBR)	
1972	B. Borg (SWEDEN)	
	C. J. Mottram (GBR)	
1973	W. Martin (USA)	
	C. S. Dowdeswell (RHODESIA)	
1974	W. Martin (USA)	
	Ash Amritraj (INDIA)	
1975	C. J. Lewis (NZ)	
	R. Ycaza (ECUADOR)	
1976	H. Guenthardt (SWITZERLAND)	
	P. Elter (GERMANY)	
1977	V. A. Winitsky (USA)	
	T. E. Teltscher (USA)	
1978	I. Lendl (CZECHOSLOVAKIA)	
	J. Turpin (USA)	
1979	R. Krishnan (INDIA)	
	D. Siegler (USA)	
1980	T. Tulasne (FRANCE)	
	H. D. Beutel (GERMANY)	

1981	M. W. Anger (USA)	
	P. Cash (AUSTRALIA)	
1982	P. Cash (AUSTRALIA)	
	H. Sundstrom (SWEDEN)	
1983	S. Edberg (SWEDEN)	
	J. Frawley (AUSTRALIA)	
1984	M.Kratzmann (AUSTRALIA)	
	S. Kruger (USA)	
1985	L. Lavalle (MEXICO)	
	E. Velez (MEXICO)	
1986	E. Velez (MEXICO)	
	J. Sanchez (SPAIN)	
1987	J. Nargiso (ITALY)	
	J. R. Stoltenberg (AUSTRALIA)	
1988	N. Pereira (VENEZUELA)	
	G. Raoux (FRANCE)	
1989	N. Kulti (SWEDEN)	
	T. A. Woodbridge (AUSTRALIA)	
1990	L. Paes (INDIA)	
	M. Ondruska (SA)	
1991	T. Enquist (SWEDEN)	
	M. Joyce (USA)	
1992	D. Skoch (CZECHOSLOVAKIA)	
	B. Dunn (USA)	
1993	R. Sabau (ROMANIA)	
	J. Szymanski (VENEZUELA)	
1994	S. Humphries (USA)	
	M. A. Philippoussis (AUSTRALIA)	
1995	O. Mutis (FRANCE)	
	N. Kiefer (GERMANY)	
1996	V. Voltchkov (BELARUS)	
	I. Ljubicic (CROATIA)	
1997	W. Whitehouse (SOUTH AFRICA)	
	D. Elsner (GERMANY)	

1998	R. Federer (SWITZERLAND)	
	I. Labadze (GEORGIA)	
1999	J. Melzer (AUSTRIA)	
	K. Pless (DENMARK)	
2000	N. Mahut (FRANCE)	
	M. Ancic (CROATIA)	
2001	R. Valent (SWITZERLAND)	
	G. Muller (LUXEMBOURG)	
2002	T. Reid (AUSTRALIA)	
	L. Quahab (ALGERIA)	
2003	F. Mergea (ROMANIA)	
	C. Guccione (AUSTRALIA)	
2004	G. Monfils (FRANCE)	
	M. Kasiri (GBR)	
2005	J. Chardy (FRANCE)	
	R. Haase (NETHERLANDS)	
2006	T. De Bakker (NETHERLANDS)	
	M. Gawron (POLAND)	
2007	D. Young (USA)	
	V. Ignatic (BELARUS)	
2008	G. Dimitrov (BULGARIA)	
	H. Kontinen (FINLAND)	
2009	A. Kuznetsov (RUSSIA)	
	J. Cox (USA)	
2010	M. Fucsovics (HUNGARY)	
	B. Mitchell (AUSTRALIA)	
2011	L. Saville (AUSTRALIA)	
	L. Broady (GBR)	

BOYS' DOUBLES

1982	P. Cash & J. Frawley	
	R. D. Leach & J. J. Ross	
1983	J. Fendick & Miss P. Hy	
	M. Nastase & O. Rahnasto	
1984	R. Brown & R. Weiss	
	M. Kratzmann & J. Svensson	
1985	A. Moreno & J. Yzaga	
	P. Korda & C. Suk	
1986	T. Carbonell & P. Korda	
	S. Barr & H. Karrasch	
1987	J. Stoltenberg & T. Woodbridge	
	D. Nargiso & E. Rossi	
1988	J. Stoltenberg & T. Woodbridge	
	D. Rikl & T. Zdrazila	
1989	J. Palmer & J. Stark	
	J-L. De Jager & W. R. Ferreira	

1990	S. Lareau & S. Leblanc	
	C. Marsh & M. Ondruska	
1991	K. Alami & G. Rusedski	
	J-L. De Jager & A. Medvedev	
1992	S. Baldas & S. Draper	
	M. S. Bhupathi & N. Kirtane	
1993	S. Downs & J. Greenhalgh	
	N. Godwin & G. Williams	
1994	B. Ellwood & M. Philippoussis	
	V. Platenik & R. Schlachter	
1995	M. Lee & J.M. Trotman	
	A. Hernandez & M. Puerta	
1996	D. Bracciali & J. Robichaud	
	D. Roberts & W. Whitehouse	
1997	L. Horna & N. Massu	
	J. Van de Westhuizen & W. Whitehouse	

1998	R. Federer & O. Rochus	
	M. Llodra & A. Ram	
1999	G. Coria & D. Nalbandian	
	T. Enev & J. Nieminen	
2000	D. Coene & K. Vliegen	
	A. Banks & B. Riby	
2001	F. Dancevic & G. Lapentti	
	B. Echagaray & S. Gonzales	
2002	F. Mergea & H. Tecau	
	B. Baker & B. Ram	
2003	F. Mergea & H. Tecau	
	A. Feeney & C. Guccione	
2004	B. Evans & S. Oudsema	
	R. Haase & V. Troicki	
2005	J. Levine & M. Shabaz	
	S. Groth & A. Kennaugh	

2006	K. Damico & N. Schnugg	
	M. Klizan & A. Martin	
2007	D. Lopez & M. Trevisan	
	R. Jebavy & M. Klizan	
2008	C-P. Hsieh & T-H. Yang	
	M. Reid & B. Tomic	
2009	P-H. Herbert & K. Krawietz	
	J. Obry & A. Puget	
2010	L. Broady & T. Farquharson	
	L. Burton & G. Morgan	
2011	G. Morgan & M. Pavic	
	O. Golding & J. Vesely	

GIRLS' SINGLES

1947	Miss G. Domken (BELGIUM)	
	Miss B. Wallen (SWEDEN)	
1948	Miss O. Miskova (CZECHOSLOVAKIA)	
	Miss V. Rigollet (SWITZERLAND)	
1949	Miss C. Mercelis (BELGIUM)	
	Miss J. S. V. Partridge (GBR)	
1950	Miss L. Cornell (GBR)	
	Miss A. Winter (NORWAY)	
1951	Miss L. Cornell (GBR)	
	Miss S. Lazzarino (ITALY)	
1952	Miss F. J. I. ten Bosch (NETHERLANDS)	
	Miss R. Davar (INDIA)	
1953	Miss D. Kilian (SA)	
	Miss V. A. Pitt (GBR)	
1954	Miss V. A. Pitt (GBR)	
	Miss C. Monnot (FRANCE)	
1955	Miss S. M. Armstrong (GBR)	
	Miss B. de Chambure (FRANCE)	
1956	Miss A. S. Haydon (GBR)	
	Miss I. Buding (GERMANY)	
1957	Miss M. Arnold (USA)	
	Miss E. Reyes (MEXICO)	
1958	Miss S. M. Moore (USA)	
	Miss A. Dmitrieva (USSR)	
1959	Miss J. Cross (SA)	
	Miss D. Schuster (AUSTRIA)	
1960	Miss K. Hantze (USA)	
	Miss L. M. Hutchings (SA)	
1961	Miss G. Baksheeva (USSR)	
	Miss K. D. Chabot (USA)	
1962	Miss G. Baksheeva (USSR)	
	Miss E. P. Terry (NZ)	
1963	Miss D. M. Salfati (FRANCE)	
	Miss K. Dening (AUSTRALIA)	

1964	Miss P. Bartkowicz (USA)	
	Miss E. Subirats (MEXICO)	
1965	Miss O. Morozova (USSR)	
	Miss R. Giscarfe (ARGENTINA)	
1966	Miss B. Lindstrom (FINLAND)	
	Miss J. A. Congdon (GBR)	
1967	Miss J. Salome (NETHERLANDS)	
	Miss E. M. Strandberg (SWEDEN)	
1968	Miss K. Pigeon (USA)	
	Miss L. E. Hunt (AUSTRALIA)	
1969	Miss K. Sawamatsu (JAPAN)	
	Miss B. I. Kirk (SA)	
1970	Miss S. Walsh (USA)	
	Miss M.V. Kroshina (USSR)	
1971	Miss M.V. Kroschina (USSR)	
	Miss S. H. Minford (GBR)	
1972	Miss I. Kloss (SA)	
	Miss G. L. Coles (GBR)	
1973	Miss A. Kiyomura (USA)	
	Miss M. Navratilova (CZECHOSLOVAKIA)	
1974	Miss M. Jausovec (YUGOSLAVIA)	
	Miss M. Simionescu (ROMANIA)	
1975	Miss N. Y. Chmyreva (USSR)	
	Miss R. Marsikova (CZECHOSLOVAKIA)	
1976	Miss N. Y. Chmyreva (USSR)	
	Miss M. Kruger (SA)	
1977	Miss L. Antonoplis (USA)	
	Miss Mareen Louie (USA)	
1978	Miss T. Austin (USA)	
	Miss H. Mandlikova (CZECHOSLOVAKIA)	
1979	Miss M. L. Piatek (USA)	
	Miss A. A. Moulton (USA)	
1980	Miss D. Freeman (AUSTRALIA)	
	Miss S. J. Leo (AUSTRALIA)	

1981	Miss Z. Garrison (USA)	
	Miss R. R. Uys (SA)	
1982	Miss C. Tanvier (FRANCE)	
	Miss H. Sukova (CZECHOSLOVAKIA)	
1983	Miss P. Paradis (FRANCE)	
	Miss P. Hy (HONG KONG)	
1984	Miss A. N. Croft (GBR)	
	Miss E. Reinach (SA)	
1985	Miss A. Holikova (CZECHOSLOVAKIA)	
	Miss J. M. Byrne (AUSTRALIA)	
1986	Miss N.M. Zvereva (USSR)	
	Miss L. Meskhi (USSR)	
1987	Miss N.M. Zvereva (USSR)	
	Miss J. Halard (FRANCE)	
1988	Miss B. Schultz (NETHERLANDS)	
	Miss E. Derly (FRANCE)	
1989	Miss A. Strnadova (CZECHOSLOVAKIA)	
	Miss M. J. McGrath (USA)	
1990	Miss A. Strnadova (CZECHOSLOVAKIA)	
	Miss K. Sharpe (AUSTRALIA)	
1991	Miss B. Rittner (GERMANY)	
	Miss E. Makarova (USSR)	
1992	Miss C. Rubin (USA)	
	Miss L. Courtois (BELGIUM)	
1993	Miss N. Feber (BELGIUM)	
	Miss R. Grande (ITALY)	
1994	Miss M. Hingis (SWITZERLAND)	
	Miss M-R. Jeon (KOREA)	
1995	Miss A. Olsza (POLAND)	
	Miss T. Tanasugarn (THAILAND)	
1996	Miss A. Mauresmo (FRANCE)	
	Miss M. L. Serna (SPAIN)	
1997	Miss C. Black (ZIMBABWE)	
	Miss A. Rippner (USA)	

1998	Miss K. Srebotnik (SLOVENIA)	
	Miss K. Clijsters (BELGIUM)	
1999	Miss I. Tulyagnova (UZBEKHISTAN)	
	Miss L. Krasnoroutskaya (USSR)	
2000	Miss M. E. Salerni (ARGENTINA)	
	Miss T. Perebiynis (UKRAINE)	
2001	Miss A. Widjaja (INDONESIA)	
	Miss D. Safina (USSR)	
2002	Miss V. Douchevina (RUSSIA)	
	Miss M. Sharapova (USSR)	
2003	Miss K. Flipkens (BELGIUM)	
	Miss A. Tchakvetadze (USSR)	
2004	Miss K. Bondarenko (UKRAINE)	
	Miss A. Ivanovic (SERBIA AND MONTENEGRO)	
2005	Miss A. Radwanska (POLAND)	
	Miss T. Paszek (AUSTRIA)	
2006	Miss C. Wozniacki (DENMARK)	
	Miss M. Rybarikova (SLOVAKIA)	
2007	Miss U. Radwanska (POLAND)	
	Miss M. Brengle (USA)	
2008	Miss L. Robson (GBR)	
	Miss N. Lertcheewakarn (THAILAND)	
2009	Miss N. Lertcheewakarn (THAILAND)	
	Miss K. Mladenovic (FRANCE)	
2010	Miss K. Pliskova (CZECH REPUBLIC)	
	Miss I. Ishizu (JAPAN)	
2011	Miss A. Barty (AUSTRALIA)	
	Miss I. Khromacheva (RUSSIA)	

GIRLS' DOUBLES

1982	Miss B. Herr & Miss P. Barg	
	Miss B. S. Gerken & Miss G. A. Rush	
1983	Miss P. Fendick & Miss P. Hy	
	Miss C. &erholm & Miss H. Olsson	
1984	Miss C. Kuhlman & Miss S. Rehe	
	Miss V. Milvidskaya & Miss L. I. Savchenko	
1985	Miss L. Field & Miss J. Thompson	
	Miss E. Reinach & Miss J. A. Richardson	
1986	Miss M. Jaggard & Miss L. O'Neill	
	Miss L. Meskhi & Miss N. M. Zvereva	
1987	Miss N. Medvedeva & Miss N.M. Zvereva	
	Miss I. S. Kim & Miss P. M. Moreno	
1988	Miss J. A. Faull & Miss R. McQuillan	
	Miss A. Dechaume & Miss E. Derly	
1989	Miss J. Capriati & Miss M. McGrath	
	Miss A. Strnadova & Miss E. Sviglerova	

1990	Miss K. Habsudova & Miss A. Strnadova	
	Miss N. J. Pratt & Miss K. Sharpe	
1991	Miss C. Barclay & Miss L. Zaltz	
	Miss J. Limmer & Miss A. Woolcock	
1992	Miss M. Avotins & Miss L. McShea	
	Miss P. Nelson & Miss J. Steven	
1993	Miss L. Courtois & Miss N. Feber	
	Miss H. Mochizuki & Miss Y. Yoshida	
1994	Miss E. De Villiers & Miss E. E. Jelfs	
	Miss C. M. Morariu & Miss L. Varmuzova	
1995	Miss C. Black & Miss A. Olsza	
	Miss T. Musgrove & Miss J Richardson	
1996	Miss O. Barabanschikova & Miss A. Mauresmo	
	Miss L. Osterloh & Miss S. Reeves	
1997	Miss C. Black & Miss I. Selyutina	
	Miss M. Matevzic & Miss K. Srebotnik	

1998	Miss E. Dyrberg & Miss J. Kostanic	
	Miss P. Rampre & Miss I. Tulyaganova	
1999	Miss D. Bedanova & Miss M.E. Salerni	
	Miss T. Perebiynis & Miss I. Tulyaganova	
2000	Miss I. Gaspar & Miss T. Perebiynis	
	Miss D. Bedanova & Miss M. E. Salerni	
2001	Miss G. Dulko & Miss A. Harkleroad	
	Miss C. Horiatopoulos & Miss B. Mattek	
2002	Miss E. Clijsters & Miss B. Strycova	
	Miss A. Baker & Miss A-L. Groenfeld	
2003	Miss A. Kleybanova & Miss S. Mirza	
	Miss K. Bohmova & Miss M. Krajicek	
2004	Miss V. Azarenka & Miss V. Havartsova	
	Miss M. Erakovic & Miss M. Niculescu	
2005	Miss V. Azarenka & Miss A. Szavay	
	Miss M. Erakovic & Miss M. Niculescu	

2006	Miss A. Kleybanova & Miss A. Pavlyuchenkova	
	Miss K. Antoniychuk & Miss A. Dulgheru	
2007	Miss A. Pavlyuchenkova & Miss U. Radwanska	
	Miss M. Doi & Miss K. Nara	
2008	Miss P. Hercog & Miss J. Moore	
	Miss I. Holl& & Miss S. Peers	
2009	Miss N. Lertcheewakarn & Miss S. Peers	
	Miss K. Mladenovic & Miss S. Njiric	
2010	Miss T. Babos & Miss S. Stephens	
	Miss I. Khromacheva & Miss E. Svitolina	
2011	Miss E. Bouchard & Miss G. Min	
	Miss D. Schuurs & Miss Hao Chen Tang	